Gifts Of Abraham

Unity
and
Peace
through
Meditation

Audi Gozlan

Copyright ©Audi Gozlan 2002
All rights reserved. No part of this book may be reproduced in any form or by any means without the prior written consent of the publisher, excepting brief quotes used in reviews.

This title is available at special quantity discounts for bulk purchases for sales promotions, premiums, fund raising, educational or institutional use. For details, contact: Ogo Books, 4613 Earnscliffe Ave.,
Montreal, PQ, H3X 2P1

First printing 2002

10 9 8 7 6 5 4 3 2 1

Printed in Canada

FIRST THOUGHTS

I have been privileged to have as my editor in chief, Rabbi Dov Baron whose unique style has contributed to the pages of this book. Dov's input has not only been in the editing but also in the development of many insights. I am grateful for his dedication toward Gifts of Abraham.

Ian Halperin of OGO books (best selling author of "Bad and Beautiful") has been the visionary of this book. I thank him for his perseverance and belief that Abraham's gifts of wisdom and meditation are a blessing to anyone searching for spirituality. Also, Deborah Jashik, Ioana Nereuta and Helene Montpetit, in the editing and organizing of this manuscript. I thank them for their involvement and commitment in making this book a reality. I am thankful to Chaim Sherff, reknown artist, for his advice and creativity. Chaim has also designed the cover depicting the Gifts of Abraham, as they arrived at the shores of India. A big thank you to David Bitton of Solika Films for putting together a video on Gifts of Abraham in a short time.

I am grateful to Simon Jacobson (author of "Towards a Meaningful Life") who has been very helpful in my showing the greatness of Abraham and his influence on mankind. Tzvi Freeman (author of "365 Meditations of the Rebbe") has provided me with ideas and advice on presenting a Jewish perspective to meditation.

Rabbi Immanuel Schochet of Toronto (author of "Mystical Concepts in Chassidism") was one of the first to have seen the manuscript and give me the encouragement necessary to make "Gifts of Abraham" a book. Rabbi Fivish Dalfin (author of "Time and Trancendence") has been instrumental in depicting the depth of meditation.

David Suissa, editor of "Olam magazine" for his constant interest and creative wisdom which has benefited this book. Meir Abehsera (author of "The Possible Man"), for teaching me how to dance with words and speak from the heart.

I am also appreciative to Rabbi Gedaliah Fleer, close friend and associate of Rabbi Aryeh Kaplan of blessed memory, author of many of the first Jewish books on meditation, Rabbi Fleer offered me valuable advice on the manuscript, in the style of Aryeh Kaplan.

The Lubavitcher Rebbe's personal secretary, Rabbi Laibel Groner who has been a great inspiration and has guided me in locating people and letters of which the Rebbe had addressed the Torah's point of view on meditation. I am thankful to Rabbi Moshe New for shedding an experienced eye on this work and providing me with many useful suggestion. During the early stages of this manuscript, Dr. Yitchak Block, philosophy professor at the University of Western Ontario, had been very encouraging in the development of an Abrahamic meditative philosophy. Rabbi Beryl Bell, Dean of the Chaya Mushka Seminary of Montreal, has been a source of "Halacha", Jewish ethics when laying out the foundations of meditation.

Close friend and spiritual advisor of Elvis Presley, Larry Gellar (best selling author of "Elvis' Search for G-d") for the many discussions we had on meditation and its place in Torah. Dan Hartal, lead actor in the documentary "Shmelvis-The Jewish Roots of Elvis", for believing in this manuscript and for your introducing me to OGO books.

Alain Malka CEO of Charles David, Marco Revah, Daniel Touizer and Arie Corcos, good friends and clients, for keeping the spiritual challenge interesting.

I extend my special appreciation to my learning partners Rabbi Naftali Pearlstein, spiritual leader of the Chai Foundation of Montreal and to Yankee Feder, a close friend since childhood . In my earlier years, I had studied in Israel and at various Yeshivahs searching for mystical meaning. I am grateful to my teachers, Rabbis Fitzi Lipsker and Dovid Wichnin, both of blessed memories, who while learning at the Morristown Yeshivah in New Jersey, taught me valuable lessons in Torah.

Rabbi Pinney Gnivish, of the Living Legacy, has been a source of inspiration on presenting the beauty of the Jewish heritage. Rabbi Noam Wagner, Rosh Yeshivah of the Lubavitch Yeshivah of Mexico City, has lead me to discovering several Chassidic teachings on meditation. Saadiah Sydney Elhadad, founder of the Yeshivah Yavne and of the Breslev Center of Montreal has provided me with good advice always needed. Rabbi Zalman Paris of Chabad of Manhattan, has offered me useful personal thoughts and experiences on meditation. Rabbi Meir Touizer, teacher and scribe in Jerusalem, has introduced me to the Sephardic teachings on meditation. Yehudah Ordower for our many discussions on Hinduism and its meditation practices.

My brother in law Moshe Esral and sister Michal for the many suggestions made. Anshel Dalfin and Rabbi Roni Autmezguine for their valuable advice. Salomon Banon and David Putterman for their creativity, and Eric Gozlan for helping spread the teachings of Jewish meditation. Steve Lazare, Ariel Cozacuru, Jack Hoziel, Valerie Azran , Ruben Lev, Victor Fadlon, Ilan Sabbah and David Dery for sharing their thoughts with me. Alain Saiman attorney, for meditating and learning with me daily at work.

As I was terminating this book in February 2002, I had learnt that my good friend Yankee Rotenstreich, who initially introduced me to my editor Dov Baron had died. I want to thank him for his encouragement, belief and confidence in publishing Gifts of Abraham.

Closest to my heart are my wife Karen and children Shamai, Geoulah, Maayan and Tsemach. You are my inspiration and reason that keep me going further. Last but not least, I honor my parents Simon and Aida Gozlan who continuously teach me great lessons in life.

The Gifts of Abraham

PART I	2
INTRODUCTION	2
Abraham's Contribution to Mankind	12
Abraham the Spiritual Rebel	19
Abraham's Legacy	26
Abraham's Sefer Yetzirah – Book of Creation	29
A New Dimension is Added to G-dly Meditation	33
Modern Day Meditation	37
The Benefits of Meditation	42
Practices of Meditation	48
Hinduism	51
Buddhism	58
Zen Buddhism	64
Taoism	70
Yoga	78
Islam's Sufism	83
Christianity	93
PART II	98
JEWISH MEDITATION	98
Jewish Meditation	99
Practicing Meditation	102
The Surroundings	102
Timing	104

   Physical Postures 107
   Initiation and Frame of Mind 109
   Avoiding Distractions 111

Soul Breathing **118**

Mastering Intellect and Emotions **126**

The State of the Body **132**

Divine Providence **141**

Pain and Suffering **152**
   The Challenge 154
   Arousing Hidden Strengths 156
   Elevating The Soul 158
   Revealing Greater Good 159

To Know G-d **163**

Creation **169**

Prayer **175**
   Prayer Exercise 179

Bonding to G-d via Torah & Mitzvoth **182**
   Mitzvah Exercise 189

Individual Mitzvoth **192**

End Note: **199**

PART I

INTRODUCTION

Introduction

It was four years ago at Montreal's Chai Center - (a youth organization catering primarily to teenagers and young adults) - that I happened to overhear several college students complain about how nothing as intense as meditation existed in Judaism. The general consensus was that even during prayer the feeling of profound spiritual connectedness they were striving to experience seemed just beyond their reach, if not completely absent. I couldn't help but interrupt them to explain the long history and relevance of meditation in Judaism. My words were met with great surprise and after an inspiring discussion, we decided to meet once a week to learn about Jewish meditation. These sessions, which continue to this day, are the inspiration for this book.

When one hears the word "meditation", various thoughts come to mind. Although people normally associate meditation with Eastern philosophies such as Yoga, Buddhism and Zen, it in fact finds its origins as far back as the days of the Old Testament and was first practiced by early biblical characters.

Abraham, our biblical forefather, used meditation as a means to discover and know G-d. Starting at a young age, he meditated regularly and discovered the essence of his Divine Soul.

Abraham taught his children and followers the power and advantages of G-dly meditation. Through his understanding of G-d, he became a master and teacher to thousands and had an effect on warriors, dignitaries, kings, and even heavenly angels.

Seven generations later, at G-d's command, Moses taught the Torah - (the Hebrew reference for the Old Testament or Bible) - to the Jewish People. Within the Torah, one can find the basis for the G-dly meditations of Abraham.

The Torah is the bedrock of Judaism. However, with the exception of a few Chassidic rabbis and Kabbalah students, most people today are unfamiliar with the subject of Jewish meditation and are pleasantly surprised to learn of its rich history, tradition and current practice. Interestingly, the Lubavitcher Rebbe – (Rabbi Menachem Mendel Schneerson) - supported and encouraged the teaching of Jewish meditation as early as the 1970s. This support was in part a response to the rising number of Jews who had begun exploring Eastern meditations.

Judaism, a religion whose relationship with G-d is based on the teachings of the Torah, offers a very intense approach to meditation. By focusing on control of the mind alone, many of the currently popular Eastern forms of meditation are primarily oriented toward relaxing the body and mind and reaching a trance state as the pathway to spiritual development. The focus of Jewish meditation, however, is G-d. In Judaism, we meditate in order to tap into our G-dly soul. With our soul power, we connect to G-d directly as He is above the physical realm and as He conceals Himself within the mundane, that is, the G-dliness implicit in all physical entities. G-dliness refers to G-d's essence as it permeates all entities, filling them with life and vitality. On this basis, the Sages of the Kabbalah describe G-d either as One who is "memale kol almin" - (fills the worlds) - or as One who is "mesovev kol almin" - (embraces the worlds). Bonding with G-d demands not only the mind and soul, but also the additional involvement of the body and emotions for optimum effect.

Like its Eastern counterparts, Jewish meditation seeks to liberate us from our physical, mental and spiritual limitations to a point where our negative emotions are in check and we are empowered to find the purpose of our daily physical existence. While some practices view the "other-worldliness" or trance state resulting from meditation as an end unto itself, in Judaism, meditation is but a means to an end. When we finally reach the point where we are free of mental, physical and spiritual limitations, we can better elicit Divine energy through the fulfillment of the Torah's Divine acts of goodness – (known as "Mitzvoth") - and make the world a place befitting that divinity.

The Mitzvoth involve prayer, study and the physical performance of actions that reinforce our relationship with the Divine. Ultimately, using our intellects suffused with "Kavanah" enhances the quality of our spiritual undertakings. Kavanah is a Hebrew word which implies deeply concentrating on our thoughts and being aware of the words we utter until the actions we convey exemplify the unity of mind and body, the unity of spiritual and physical and the unity of the material with the Divine. Hence, regardless of your meditative preference, the Jewish approach to meditation offers insight on how to further enhance the quality of meditative experiences by including all aspects of existence.

The most common form of Jewish meditation is prayer. Like "mantra meditation", "davening" - (the Yiddish word for worship) - implies the repetition of certain holy verses several times daily. One such repetition is the "Amida", a prayer consisting of eighteen blessings recited three times a day – at dawn, in the afternoon and again at night. The Talmud[1] explains that the Chassidim Harishonim - (the early Chassidic people who lived during the era of the first temple) - would meditate for at least one hour each morning before and after prayer. On this basis, Maimonides explains in his Tract on Prayer that by meditating we can clear our minds and allow for the perception of the Shechinah, G-d's Divine presence.

Yet, there is a lot more to Jewish meditation than what one can achieve during the course of prayer. Memorizing a page of Talmud - (ancient oral tradition put in writing between the years 200 BCE to 300 CE) - can cause an elevating feeling both mentally and spiritually. Similarly, the G-dly act of the giving of charity can be an electrifying experience between the giver and taker. Partaking in a traditional brotherly dance in which everyone holds hands and moves tightly in a perfect circle creates a state of happiness and unity[2]. Each of these lofty forms of meditation requires Kavanah, as discussed above, for paramount effect.

Another popular ritual, the singing of contemplative melodies at a Chassidic farbrengen - (gathering) - is simply meditation by another name. On such occasions, the sounds cascading throughout the synagogue and the voices vibrating from within carry one to a reverie in which memory and thought similarly surface from within.

In Lubavitch Chassidic tradition, on special occasions and at least once a month a Chassidic discourse is memorized and then recited before a group of listeners during the course of a farbrengen. This has been a practice of the Chassidic Masters, usually referred to as Rebbes, since the time of the Baal Shem Tov, the founder of Chassidism[3] - (1689-1760).

It is said that when a Rebbe delivers such a discourse, he is imbued with a Divine energy and inspiration akin to the highest meditative achievement. The preparation and recital of the discourse is a high form of meditation. The energy and feeling of exuberance caused by the study of a Chassidic discourse can only be appreciated through personal experience.

In the late 1970s, Rabbi Aryeh Kaplan, together with psychiatrists and psychologists, formulated the first modern-day guidelines to Jewish meditation. In his book <u>Jewish Meditation</u>[4], Rabbi Kaplan deals largely with the methods of Rabbi Nachman of Breslov, a Chassidic master well known for his practices and teachings on meditation.

Immediately after the publication of Rabbi Kaplan's books on meditation, many groups in the United States and Israel began practicing and experimenting with Jewish meditation.

Others who have advanced and taught about Jewish meditation are Rabbi Louis Jacobs, Rabbi Zalman Schachter-Shalomi and Rabbi Shlomo Carlbach.

Many books on Jewish mysticism have been adapted and published in English, French and many other languages.

Some of these books are based on the great Jewish classics of the Maimonides, the Baal Shem Tov, the Vilna Gaon, Rabbi Nachman of Breslov, Rabbi Schneur Zalman of Liadi, and the Ramchal. Once available only in Hebrew, a full library of these teachings can now be accessed in many languages. Covering a wide range of topics such as the path to happiness and meaning, Divine Providence and turning spiritual thought into action, these manuscripts offer important insight on Jewish meditation.

To realize our greatest hopes and aspirations, we must grapple with the challenge of bridging the gap between thought and action. Given that overcoming such a challenge necessitates a physical manifestation along with intellectual and emotional inspiration, a meditative exercise that strengthens the mind alone and denies the contribution of the body and the emotions to spiritual endeavors will not sufficiently prepare us for this daunting transformation. It is in this manner that the Torah's meditation practices are unique.

The teachings of Chassidic philosophy offer guidance on this age-old dilemma. Rabbi Schneur Zalman, founder of Chabad[5] Chassidism, focused his teachings primarily on bringing thought into action. His most famous work, <u>Tanya</u>, has been printed in many languages and is available internationally. This book presents in a comprehensible way the essential elements of Jewish meditation as depicted in the mystical teachings of the Kabbalah.

With the advent of the new millennium, more people than ever before are seeking the path of spiritual growth and enlightenment. People of all faiths, ages and from all walks of life hunger for alternative sources of empowerment and solutions to the problems of daily life. Frustrated and drained by the high expectations and subsequent disappointments associated with the demands of modern life, many people feel an internal void and can isolate neither its cause nor its cure. While modern medicine has yet to offer a panacea for the nagging feelings of emptiness that many people encounter, meditation renews us physically and spiritually by allowing us to experience other-worldliness, clarity of thought and relaxation.

More and more, people are realizing that the cure for what ails them is not always found in a medical prescription. Alternative medicines and the therapeutic exercise of meditation now play an important role in complementing standard medical practice. People are becoming more health conscious, many changing their diets to macrobiotic, semi-biotic, vegetarian or all protein. Many practices once considered radical or stigmatized as being "alternative", are now considered the "in" thing to do and are being passionately embraced by attorneys, businessmen, politicians, housewives and teenagers with equal intensity.

Over the years, I have come to realize that meditation works – even without sitting in a yoga position. What is wonderful about meditation is that its philosophy is not all that complicated. You don't have to be a guru or a spiritual leader to be able to meditate. In simple terms, one needs but to focus inward and control one's thoughts. Obviously, this is more easily said than done.

Meditation necessitates a lot of work and practice. Just as some artists may be satisfied with the creation of a few simple sketches, others wish to thoroughly absorb and express the subtleties of the subject, allowing their passionate interpretations to explode onto the canvas. In meditation as in art, practice, knowledge, intent and concentration will together determine how deeply we can reach within ourselves and the quality of the end result. Whether we create a superficial sketch or a masterpiece that captures the soul of our subject depends on our intentions, our daily needs, and, of course, our curiosity. With practice and understanding of its subtleties, meditation allows us to reach into the deepest, purest recesses of our soul - the source of Divine creativity. We can simply close our eyes and concentrate on our breathing while sitting in a comfortable position or we can reach loftier levels by focusing, for example, on how G-d has filled us with Divine energy through His infinite light.

Although G-d is neither male nor female, for the sake of uniformity, I have referred to the Al-mighty in the masculine throughout this book. Also, I have avoided spelling the name G-d in its entirety, spelling it instead with a hyphen, in keeping with Torah law. Because the Divine name is holy and must be treated with the greatest care and respect it is spelled in full only in holy books such as a prayer book or bible.

My hope is that this book will help the reader discover, strengthen and concretize his or her internal resources, virtuous thoughts and aspirations. To truly gain from these teachings, one must be willing to practice meditation on a daily basis. Not limited to certain periods of the day, meditation is more a way of thinking and living, and can be practiced while immersed in our daily routines.

In bringing to light the history and relevance of Abraham's meditations as practiced in the Torah, this book will discuss among others, Yoga, Buddhist and Zen Buddhist philosophies. I was initially introduced to Eastern types of meditation about twenty years ago by a close friend - Yehudah. He later moved to India with his family, but at the time, held meditation gatherings in his home and at the ashram he attended. With his encouragement, I learned about the ancient practices of meditation. My experiences with Yehudah only ignited my inspiration to explore the role of meditation in Judaism more thoroughly. Thankfully, my understanding, passion and practice of Jewish meditation and mysticism blossomed more than I had ever dreamed possible.

Ultimately, I hope to acquaint you with the historically relevant and spiritually rewarding Torah approach to meditation. Since meditation is a means of attaining spirituality, one may be surprised to learn that Jewish meditation, at least outwardly, resembles that of Eastern religions. In fact, the Zohar[6] originally elucidated the similarities between Eastern forms of meditation and those of the Jewish tradition. While the Zohar acknowledges these foreign practices, however, it also cautions against their misuse. Hence, for the sake of clarity, perspective and comparison, I will discuss Eastern philosophies in relation to Jewish mysticism and meditation alone.

It is my hope that those who may have tasted other waters will see that within the Torah's tradition, one can discover a well of genuine wisdom capable of satisfying anyone's thirst.

"There is nothing new under the sun" is an axiom of our Sages. After the devastating September 11th terrorist attacks on America, the world is visibly shaken and searching for new purpose and meaning. I believe that the world would become a better place to live if more people looked back to our forefather Abraham and learned about his teachings.

Abraham was not only a great thinker and philosopher, but also a man of action. When the time came to challenge crimes against humanity, he stood at the forefront. Living in an age of immorality, corruption and terror, Abraham understood that the only solution was to recall the elements of humanity. He encouraged his generation to have a sincere concern for the welfare of mankind and to become more G-dly. For this reason, they called him "enlightened one".

If the world learned Abraham's lessons of tolerance, concern for others and faith in a merciful G-d, the course of history would finally change and the world would experience real peace. Abraham, in his time, succeeded in positively affecting his country of birth Iraq and, later on, the Middle East, where he lived until the end of his days. One of Abraham's greatest accomplishments was his influence on the countries of the East, where he sent his sons with ethereal gifts of wisdom. Abraham's teachings tremendously affected our past and could definitely shape our future.

Introduction

Whenever and wherever he traveled, Abraham disseminated G-dliness. Every person he met, he taught that there is one G-d and it is befitting to serve him. He would sojourn from city to city and from country to country gathering people together and teaching them about G-d's existence. Don't let a moment go by without sharing your light!

Chapter 1
Abraham's Contribution to Mankind

Abraham, our forefather, was probably the first person to have practiced meditation regularly. In fact, he began to meditate at the age of three when he discovered G-d and the presence of his Divine Soul.

Abraham lived thirty-eight centuries ago. At the age of seventy-five, he was commanded by G-d: *"Lech Lecha" – "Go for yourself"*. Understanding these words simply, Abraham left his country and his birthplace.

However, the Torah's usage of the words *"Lech Lecha"*, literally translated as *"Go to you"*, also implies a movement towards one's true purpose and self. Abraham was being commanded to journey beyond his limited frame of reference to discover his unlimited connection to the Divine, the spark of G-d that forms the soul of every human being. When a person connects to his or her inner-self, there is no limit to that person's potential for growth.

Interestingly, the whole known history of Abraham began to unfold with this one commandment as recorded in the Torah. No details of his background are found in the Torah, except that he was born, married, and that he traveled with his father from Ur to Canaan. The fact that the Torah saw fit to begin with this particular narrative about Abraham is indicative of its central importance.

Inspired by this first commandment, Abraham saw fit to teach and transmit to others the significance of the soul as a legacy for all of his children. Abraham was the first to teach us of the higher aspect of humanity, the "inner self" – the soul of man that is a part of G-d, free of all mental and emotional obstacles and confinements.

Throughout history, many have believed that developing an objective mind, controlling one's thoughts and developing intuition are skills necessary to attain high levels of accomplishment. Yet our ability to reach such high levels of objectivity, intuition and concentration is hindered by the limited nature of the mind, and the constant war raging between our intellect and our emotions.

At times, it is as if the mind has a mind of its own, an interfering thought process or voice that reminds us of our physical limitations and deficiencies. The harder we try to control our minds, the more they refuse to be dominated. When we try to focus on one thought, our minds drift to another. Thus, when faced with a trying situation, the mind often is the epicenter of conflicting thoughts. On the one hand, our natural impulses may motivate us to react in one way, while on the other hand our cool intellect will cause us to perceive and react to the same situation in a totally different manner.

The practice of meditation forces us to exorcise our mental demons through the exercise of concentration until we reach a level of silent other-worldliness where clarity, objectivity and intuition reign supreme. Meditation can be defined as the cessation of the mental process, whereby the mind ends its internal conversation. When the mind becomes clear of all thoughts, it is free to experience and sense the G-dly soul within. When we reach the unity of mind with G-d, the power of the mind is no longer limited and we can even visualize future events[7].

The very first reference to this type of visualization is found in the book of Genesis, when G-d tells Abraham to go outside his tent, look toward the heavens and count the stars. G-d then makes a covenant with Abraham promising him that his children will be as many as the stars of the sky and that his future will be prosperous.

Meditation provides us with clarity of vision akin to the bright sky that illuminated Abraham's vision and allowed him to visualize his descendants on that night long ago. Had the sky been cloudy, Abraham would have been as blind to the beauty of the heavens as we are to our true consciousness when the mind is clouded by thoughts and images. Just as the clear sky and shining stars enabled Abraham to visualize his future descendants as promised by G-d, with a clear mind produced by meditation we are enabled to visualize our own future.

Today's major religious movements emanate from Abraham's children. The Jewish People are the descendants of Isaac, as the Muslims are from Ishmael, the Christians, Catholics and Protestants from Abraham's grandson Esau (the ancestor of Rome) and the Eastern religions from Abraham's six later sons, Zimran, Yakshan, M'dan, Midyan, Yishbak and Shoach.

The Torah tells us that at the age of one hundred and forty, Abraham married a woman named Ketura. Ketura, also known as Hagar, was the daughter of an Egyptian Pharaoh. Recognizing Abraham's great wisdom and knowledge of G-d, Hagar so strongly wished to become a part of his household that she became a maidservant to Abraham's first wife, Sarah. Later, she became Abraham's second wife by Sarah's consent. However, due to a conflict between Sarah and Hagar, Abraham divorced Hagar and sent her away when her son Ishmael reached the age of thirteen.

After leaving his household, Hagar rebelled against Abraham's beliefs by reverting to the idol worship of her upbringing. Later, she repented and G-d renamed her "Ketura". According to the Sages[8], she was renamed Ketura because her deeds were as sweet as the Ketoret, the incense offering in the Holy Temple.

After Sarah's passing, G-d commanded Abraham to take Ketura back into his household. After they remarried, Ketura bore Abraham six sons, all of whom Abraham circumcised as commanded by G-d[9]. He hoped that the holy covenant he established on their skin would always remind them of their exclusive spiritual relationship with the one G-d he had come to know.

None, however, followed the spiritual path of Abraham's monotheism; instead, all six sons became idol worshippers and practitioners of the black arts. In fact, the Midrash tells us that their names reflect their deeds. For example, the name Zimran suggests "singer to idols", while Yakshan implies "drummer to idols", etc.

The Torah tells us that when Abraham saw that the sons he fathered with Ketura were veering from the path of the One Creator G-d, he sent them away to the "Land of the East[10]" – (the biblical reference for India). Why India? Perhaps it was their own choice, thinking that in India they would find spiritual and physical freedom. Or perhaps it was Abraham's hope that his sons could greatly contribute to the spiritual development of this Eastern land. Interestingly, India, in Hebrew, is called "Hodu", which also means to praise, sing or worship.

Sending his children away from home was probably very painful for Abraham. Upon their departure, he gave them part of his most treasured assets – gifts of wisdom and spiritual powers that he had acquired over the years. The Talmud states[11] that these gifts were "Shem HaTumah". They included deep secrets of meditation and contemplation through which they could reach enlightenment.

Seeing that his sons were heading towards a life of idolatry, Abraham gave them these "gifts" for protection. He was optimistic that through the enlightenment engendered by them, his sons would one day return to the faith of their father. Instead, these gifts opened their eyes to the "Sitra Achra[12]", spiritual powers in opposition to Abraham's mission of cultivating an environment that honored the one G-d, the Creator of the Universe.

Interestingly, these gifts called "Shem HaTumah" by Abraham are explained as the art of black magic and alternative modes of spirituality by the 11th century commentator, Rashi. Later, the Hindus adopted the word "tames", into their everyday language and use it in association with black magic and witchcraft[13]. The word "tames" in Hebrew is a variation of the word "tumah", of Shem Ha Tumah as mentioned above.

The 15th century philosopher Rabbi Menashe Ben Israel explained the influence Abraham had on the teachings of the East as follows[14]:

> *"Similarly, ... he sent the sons of his concubines away from Isaac while he was yet alive towards the East – to their holy land, India. They also disseminated this faith. Behold, you may see there the Abrahamites, who are today called Brahmans; they are the sons of Abraham our patriarch and they were the first in India to spread this faith, as Apollonius Tionius, who spoke with them and King Yercha face to face, testified... And they spoke the truth, for from the seed of Abraham this ideology was created anew. From there, the new belief spread all over India, as is evident from the writings of that period. Their faith is, however, often thought of as Pythagoras' innovation, since it had disappeared for a few years, but he was not the originator. Also, this was the code followed by Alexander Polister who heard and studied it from the prophet Ezekiel who was his mentor."*

Abraham's son Isaac, however, was his prime spiritual successor. Isaac remained in his father's monotheist path and received the full wisdom of his father, which would later become inscribed in the Torah. The duty of performing the "Avoda[15]", the service to G-d, was given specifically to Isaac.

Having enjoyed close relationships with his father Abraham and half-brother Isaac throughout his childhood, Ishmael retained his father's monotheistic beliefs despite Hagar's earlier expulsion and rebellion. This intimate, long-term and historically relevant relationship between Ishmael, Abraham and Isaac further elucidates why today many people consider Arabs and Jews to be "cousins" despite the disparity in the religions they practice.

In contrast to Isaac and Ishmael, Abraham's other children received only the gifts of "Shem HaTumah" which contributed to the formation of the Eastern meditative religions we know today. In chapters 9-15, we will discuss the striking similarities and differences between several meditative religions and Judaism.

Abraham was commanded to sojourn above the frontiers of his intellect and establish an infinite connection with G-d. And thus he built an ever-blossoming bridge between G-d and His creations, one founded not on intellect, but on our infinite capacity to love and trust in the Almighty.

Chapter 2
Abraham the Spiritual Rebel

From the Midrash, we learn the story of Abraham's youth. Many important lessons can be derived from the early experiences of the father of meditation.

Abraham was born in the year 1812 BCE in the city of Ur, Mesopotamia, today known as Iraq. His father Terach was a government minister and idol merchant.

During this period, the masses practiced polytheism, worshipping the sun, moon, and many statues believed to possess supernatural powers. Even Nimrod, the cunning ruler at the time, claimed to be a god. He dealt very harshly with anyone who doubted his divinity.

Nimrod's astrologers prophesized that a male child would be born who would one day challenge his throne. They predicted that this child would deny Nimrod's claim of divinity and denounce the worship of other supposedly powerful gods.

Nimrod asked his advisors what measures should be taken to guard against this threat. Their solution was to annihilate all newborn boys. Nimrod readily agreed. He ordered that special houses be built to hospitalize all women in labor. There, the newborn boys would be separated from the girls and killed.

Terach, an honored advisor of Nimrod, had recently fathered a son whom he had named Abram. Terach, who had been present during the meeting with the astrologers, asked Nimrod whether his newborn son would be included in the edict. The ruler reassured Terach, explaining that his son was exempt since Terach was so trusted in his eyes.

The decree was promptly enforced and thousands of newborn boys were slaughtered. After the horrific fact, Nimrod's astrologers continued to see imminent danger. They told Nimrod of a star they saw above the house of Terach, shooting out in all directions of the heavens and overpowering the stars from the East, West, North and South. This astrological vision implicated Terach's newborn son Abram as the one destined to challenge Nimrod's divinity.

Nimrod immediately ordered that Abram be put to death. When Terach became aware of the order, he told his wife Amtalai to wrap the baby and hide him in a cave far from their home. When Nimrod's agents came to take Abram, Terach pretended to cooperate with them, but instead handed over the newly born son of his maidservant.

Thus, Abram spent the first ten years of his life in the cave where his mother had hidden him. During the many hours and days of seclusion from the corrupt world around him, Abram came to know G-d through meditation and contemplation while he observed the movement of the sun, the moon, the stars and the earth around him.

At first Abram reasoned: *"Maybe I should worship the earth, since it is the earth's produce that sustains all living beings"*. Then he thought: *"The earth is not all so powerful, for it depends on the rain to grow its produce"*. Then it occurred to him that perhaps he should prostrate himself to the firmament. *"The sun"*, he assumed, *"must be the most powerful one in the heavens, since it provides the world with light and warmth."* But night came and the sun disappeared, giving way to the moon. He then supposed that the moon was the genuine "all-powerful" one, since it seemed to overpower the sun. This thought came to a quick end when he saw that the moon only glowed at night.

Abram meditated on all the natural forces of the world, the rhythms of night and day, the seasons and the many ecological systems. He came to understand the patterns and cycles of creation known to us as Nature and in Hebrew called "teva". After much contemplation, the wise young Abram[16] concluded that there must be a higher power dictating and vitalizing all the forces of Nature. He recognized that the stars, the moon and the sun have no will of their own. He realized that they are merely instruments of the One G-d who animates them as they carry out their duties of traveling in their orbits and transmitting warmth and light.

Abram understood that G-d was invisible, stating:
"I have not seen Him, but I can understand that only a mighty and merciful G-d could have created this marvelous world around me, and only His superior intelligence is able to keep it going. To Him shall I bow[17]."

Following this self-enlightenment, G-d revealed Himself to Abram and showed him the true way of worshipping Him. Abraham later studied at the acclaimed school of Shem and Ever – (descendants of Noah) - meditating and learning about G-d and His wisdom for many more years.

After some time had passed and it appeared that the prediction of the new star did not come to fruition, Abram returned home to Ur.

As mentioned earlier, Abram's father Terach was in the business of trading idols. Abram, who already knew that only G-d was the true Al-mighty, did everything he could to dissuade the polytheistic Mesopotamians from their idolatrous beliefs. Although the charismatic young Abram persuaded many of his father's customers that their faith in idols was false, he could not convince his stubborn father.

The Midrash[18] describes how one day, a woman brought a bowl of fresh flour as an offering for Terach's idols. Abram was tending his father's idol store at the time, as Terach was away. After the woman left, Abram took an ax and destroyed the entire collection of idols except for the largest one. He then placed the ax by the largest idol's side. When his father returned and found the shattered idols, he blamed Abram for the damages.

Abram denied responsibility for the damages, saying that the idols had argued over an offering brought for them. He told his father that the biggest idol had become very offended and had destroyed all of the smaller idols in anger.

Terach exclaimed that such a thing was impossible since the idols were made of wood and stone and could not speak or move. Realizing that his son had succeeded in having him admit that his idols were powerless, Terach reported Abram to Nimrod.

Nimrod immediately had Abram arrested and imprisoned. This was the first of ten trials[19] Abram was to face. At all costs, Abram bravely rejected all forms of deity besides the One G-d, Creator of the Universe.

After ten years of imprisonment, Nimrod condemned Abram to death by fire in the city of Ur Kasdim. Abram had ridiculed Nimrod's deification of fire. As retribution, Abram was to be punished by this supposed deity.

Hundreds of people gathered to watch the prince of Terach burned alive for his disrespect of Nimrod's gods. Prior to being placed in the great burning furnace, Abram announced to all the people gathered that G-d was the only Great Power in the world and no one, including Nimrod, could challenge His authority. He proclaimed that the fire could not harm him unless G-d so desired – for G-d, who gave fire the strength to burn, could take that strength away. Rumors of Abram's inspirational words spread quickly amongst the people as they eagerly anticipated the results of his trial by fire.

Abram was thrown into the great fiery furnace. To everyone's astonishment, Abram walked away from the furnace after three days, without even a single hair singed. As he stepped out of the fire, his first words were: *"The G-d who created heaven and earth, against whom you have rebelled, has saved me from death"*.

Nimrod immediately prostrated himself before Abram and was followed by all of his ministers. Abram told them to stand, for one must only bow to G-d and no one else. Nimrod finally admitted that Abram was indeed an "exalted one", a man of G-d who spoke only the truth.

After this incident thousands of people became followers of Abram, joining him and his community in pursuit of enlightenment and knowledge of G-d. Abram became a renowned leader, mentor and teacher.

It is interesting to note that the name "Abram" consists of the two words "Ab" which in Hebrew means "father" or "leader", and "ram" which means "the elevated one". In Hindu, "Ram" refers to an elevated deity. Similarly, in the eyes of the Mesopotamians, Abram was viewed as an exalted G-dly being.

Abram's camp is probably the first historical appearance of an "Ashram[20]". Interestingly, the Torah cites the name of Abram's great-grandson as "Ashurim", while the commentator Onkelos translates the name Ashurim as a "camp" or "community". It is likely that Abram's great-grandson Ashurim spread the concept of the spiritual Ashram to the East.

Although they had witnessed the truth of the One Creator G-d through the miracle of Abram, the majority of Mesopotamians continued to worship all types of idols.

When Abram reached the age of ninety-nine, G-d appeared to him and changed his name from "Abram" to "Abraham", adding the additional Hebrew letter Hei to his name.

The Torah commentator Rashi explains that while Abram means father of Aram, Abraham in Hebrew is an acronym for Av Hamon Goyim – father of many nations. This change alludes to Abraham's ability to inspire people of all nations to meditate on and connect with G-d, the Creator of the Universe.

The addition of the letter Hei, which has the Hebrew numerical value of five, to his name also signifies that Abraham had gained control over five additional senses. Since the day he discovered G-d, Abraham learned to control and focus his mind, emotions and bodily functions through meditation and contemplation. At the ripe age of ninety-nine, Abraham was so advanced that he could fully control his entire physical existence, including the organs that are normally impossible to dominate – the two ears, the two eyes and the membrum.

Heaven is not just a place we will eventually encounter as a reward for good deeds done. Indeed if we would just carry goodness into our daily life, we would be bringing heaven down to earth today.

Chapter 3
Abraham's Legacy

Abraham had a large tent in the midst of a desert and always invited travelers to eat and lodge in the comfort of his home. He would serve people food and drink and see to all of their other needs. When people wanted to thank and bless him, he would encourage them to instead praise and bless the "One who spoke and the world came into being". After this eye-opening request, many of Abraham's guests stayed on to learn more about G-d and His ways.

Talmudic Sages[21] believe that in the following text from Genesis 21:33: *"And he (Abraham) called there on the name of G-d, master of the world"*, the Hebrew word used to mean "And he called" in fact implies something far greater. They comment: *"Do not read Vayikra – and he called, rather Vayakri – and he caused others to call."* In other words, Abraham's mission in life, through his acts of kindness to others, was to bring people to know G-d as the provider and creator of all physical existence.

Abraham was often called the "Ivri". In Hebrew, Ivri means "outsider", referring to his spiritual rebelliousness. While Abraham practiced monotheism, the rest of his generation believed in polytheism. The cognomen "Ivri" later became the basis of the word "Jew". It is possible that the Indus River in India was named after Abraham, since Indus means "the outcast" in Indian.

During his life, Abraham's wisdom spread throughout the known world. He was looked upon as a great spiritual leader and a great philosopher. He was also very wealthy and practiced great generosity. He regularly spoke with extraterrestrial beings and even with G-d. On at least one occasion, he had angels dine at his table.

Although he had many servants and workers, Abraham insisted on personally caring for his flock of sheep. This activity was very important to Abraham, as it allowed him the opportunity to meditate for long hours without interruption.

Abraham's traditions, spirituality and appreciation of G-d were passed on as a legacy to his children. Yet, there are important distinctions to be made between the way Isaac and the rest of Abraham's sons received his traditions.

Isaac continued in the path of his father Abraham by studying in the Torah academy of Shem and Ever. He spent much of his time meditating and contemplating a single G-d as Creator of the Universe and influencing others to do the same. In contrast, Isaac's brothers, except for Ishmael, were sent off to the "Land of the East" or India, where, as new immigrants, they were known as "Abrahamites".

It was through Isaac that Abraham faced G-d's greatest test. G-d commanded Abraham to sacrifice his son Isaac to Him on an altar. At the last moment, G-d sent an angel to stop Abraham. Our Sages say that Isaac remained an "Olah Temimah", a perfect sacrifice throughout his life. In order to preserve this holiness, Isaac never left the Holy Land.

In many ways, Isaac had an even closer bond with G-d than did his father. Abraham conceived Isaac after he had been circumcised as commanded by G-d. Abraham himself did not have this advantage, as his father Terach had not been commanded to circumcise himself. Thus, it was not necessary for G-d to test Isaac with many trials and tribulations as He had tested his father Abraham.

Isaac was also the father of Jacob, from who came the twelve tribes and the Jewish Nation of Israel. The Talmud[22] states that in the World-To-Come we shall say specifically of Isaac: *"For you are our father"*. So, as Abraham became the "father of many nations", Isaac became the father of the Jewish People.

Like an architect He looked upon His blueprints - "the five books" - and created the world. Every word He spoke brought existence into the universe. We, the builders, have the duty of maintaining His masterpiece.

Chapter 4
Abraham's Sefer Yetzirah – Book of Creation

Many of Abraham's thoughts about G-d and Creation are found in the book he authored, Sefer Yetzirah – the Book of Creation[23]. Sefer Yetzirah may be the oldest book in the world on mysticism. At present, at least four versions of Sefer Yetzirah exist: the short version, the long version, the Saadia Gaon version, and the version of the Vilna Gaon, Rabbi Eliyahu.

The work is essentially divided into four general chapters. In chapter one, Abraham introduces the "Sefirot" - the Divine attributes involved in the creation of the world. In chapter two, he discusses the significance of the Hebrew alphabet and its mystical powers in relation to the creation of the world. As we read in the above passage, the entire universe was created through letters of speech, and its existence is dependent on their constant repetition. We shall discuss this in more detail in Chapter 22.

In chapters three, four and five, he elaborates on the various aspects and features of the Hebrew letters - the original language of the Bible. The Midrash states[24]: *"The letters were given to none other than Abraham"*. There, he explains that the letters are divided into "mothers", "doubles" and "elementals" which are connected to the "universe", "soul" and "year". It is very probable that the astrological arrangements were influenced by these teachings.

The final chapter of Abraham's Sefer Yetzirah is considered to be one of the most mystical and obscure writings in Hebrew literature. The topics and ideas are completely original and appear to have no connection whatsoever with the previous chapters. Terms not found in the Torah such as "teli" (axis), "galgal" (cycle), and "lev" (heart), are introduced in this chapter. These concepts, described in an obscure manner, are thought to explore the latitude, angles and cycles of the world, as well as paths to wisdom.

The last chapter of Sefer Yetzirah states:

"And when Abraham our father gazed, looked, saw, delved, understood, engraved, carved, permuted and depicted, he was successful. And the Master of All, Blessed be He, revealed Himself to him, and took him in His bosom (kissed him on the head, and called him, "My beloved"). He made a covenant of circumcision – and between the ten fingers of his hands – this is the covenant of the tongue. He bound the twenty-two letters to his tongue and revealed their foundation. He drew them in water, burned them in fire, and agitated them with breath. He ignited them with the seven (planets), and directed them with the twelve constellations[25]."

Coincidentally, the mystical Veda scriptures date back to the 18th century BCE, not long after Abraham's Sefer Yetzirah came to the fore. This congruence of dates and the strong theoretical similarities of the two books further highlight Abraham's probable influence on Hinduism. In chapter 9, we will compare the Veda's view of Creation to that of the Kabbalah.

The Talmud[26] tells us that Abraham also authored a second book consisting of 400 chapters covering worship of the occult. It has been suggested that this work is part of the wisdom that Abraham gave to his children when he sent them off to the East.

When reading the Sefer Yetzirah, one observes that it is a meditative work containing many mystical secrets. According to tradition, the book offers a recipe for the creation of a living being. Through the secrets of the Sefer Yetzirah, the Maharal of Prague – (an ancient eminent Jewish mystic) - is said to have created a spiritual android, known in Hebrew as a "Golem", to protect his Jewish community against the blood libels frequently terrorizing them.

According to some commentators[27], when the Torah states that *"Abraham took... the souls which he made in Haran...28,"* this actually means that Abraham created individuals through the mystical powers of the Sefer Yetzirah.

Throughout the generations, Abraham's descendants often made use of the mystical powers of the Sefer Yetzirah. It is said that the eldest sons of Jacob created animals and maidservants through it[29]. Moreover, when the Israelites left Egypt, Betzalel was commanded to build the Tabernacle for G-d in the desert. The Talmud[30] explains that he was chosen for this most holy task since he *"knew how to permute the letters with which heaven and earth were created"*, a skill he learned from studying the Sefer Yetzirah[31].

Since the beginning of creation, a part of the world has been patiently waiting for you to come and redeem it. Ever since your soul was formed, it has been eagerly waiting to descend into your body to fulfill its holy task. Ask yourself: "Have I found my part"!

Chapter 5
A New Dimension is Added to G-dly Meditation

Several hundred years after Abraham wrote the Sefer Yetzirah, G-d appeared to his Hebrew[32] descendants on Mount Sinai and gave them the Torah. With this great revelation, a significant change occurred in the way the world connected with G-d.

The Sages explain[33] that according to Psalms 115:16: *"The heavens are the heavens of G-d, but the earth He gave to the children of man"*. Hence, initially, the physical realm was separated from the spiritual by Divine decree. Material existence prevented one from truly appreciating spiritual reality. Thus, prior to the giving of the Torah, one could only perceive G-d through abstract means by separating one's self from the physical or material realm.

After the giving of the Torah, G-d nullified this "decree" and allowed for a true unity to exist between the material and the spiritual. The Torah says: *"And the Eternal came down upon Mount Sinai[34]"* and to Moses, G-d said: *"Come up to the Eternal[35]"*. From the time that G-d's essence was first revealed to man through the giving of the Torah, we have been able to reach and unite with the very essence of G-d or "Ein Sof" - (Eternal Light) - by physically fulfilling His commandments.

Prior to the experience on Mount Sinai, mankind could bond with G-d only spiritually, through meditation and contemplation. After the Torah was given, man was empowered to draw G-d into the world through physical means and objects on a permanent basis, allowing for a true unity of body and soul. Thus, the role and practice of meditation was forever changed after the Torah was given.

Although they were not yet commanded to fulfill the edicts of the Torah, the forefathers did indeed observe G-d's decrees – (mitzvoth) - but only in a spiritual way. For example, the Zohar[36] explains how Jacob used alternate methods to elicit the spiritual light usually attained by fulfilling the later decreed mitzvah of wearing tefillin – (Holy Scriptures in leather boxes worn by Jews during morning prayers)[37].

The purpose of the Torah was to establish a permanent abode for G-d within a physical world through the performance of mitzvoth – (physical acts of goodness as dictated in the Torah). According to the Jewish faith, the world's continued existence is dependent on the fulfillment of mitzvoth, as through their fulfillment a great flow of life is drawn into the world from G-d, the Source of Life. We will discuss the mitzvoth in the context of meditation in chapters 24 and 25.

Abraham's sons, who went off to Eastern countries before the Torah was given, were familiar with the pre-Torah school of thought – meditation in the abstract without tangible and permanent physical effects. For them, spiritual enlightenment and meditation were more intellectual than physical exercises, focusing on separation of the body from the world rather than the unification of the two. Even though the descendants of Isaac's brothers, many of whom were living in the East, did not receive the Torah and had no knowledge of the mitzvoth, they were still given the Seven Laws of Noah which are shared with all of mankind. Maimonides explains - (Laws of Kings ch. 89) - that these rules of humanity were developed by Adam, Noah and then Abraham[38].

Indeed various styles of meditation are commendable and effective. Still, if any one of them does not fulfill the Divine intent of spiritualizing the world, then it has not venerated the Torah. Hence, many meditative and spiritual practices are different from the Torah's, since they are practiced in the abstract and promote separation from worldly existence.

Interestingly, some meditative styles that exist today are attractive precisely due to the fact that they mostly repudiate involvement with the material. They are believed to penetrate more deeply into the unconscious. In contrast, the Torah requires that our meditations translate into physical realities. For this reason, the Torah provides mitzvoth that involve physical activity; these are misconstrued by some as being superficial for this very reason.

As G-d desired a spiritual dwelling place within this physical world, only through our combined intellectual, physical and emotional manifestation of His Divine Will can we serve Him, the Cause of the world's existence. Meditation oriented on the abstract and intellectual alone can only bring us halfway along the path to true spiritual enlightenment, simply because it ignores the important role of the physical and the emotional.

According to Judaism, the mitzvoth are our G-d given tools through which we can connect the spiritual with the physical and live more meaningful lives. Through the performance of mitzvoth, we elevate ourselves, our surroundings and even mankind as a whole to a level where all have a direct link with G-d. When physical mitzvoth are enhanced by the correct meditations, the combined effect of physical and intellectual practice will lead us to our spiritual destination.

Enlightenment is dependent on our Divine efforts. Normally beyond the grasp of mortals, true enlightenment can only be reached through our own initiative. We have been endowed with this skill. Have you made the effort yet?

Jewish form of meditation as an alternative to some Eastern meditative practices beckoning many Jews to a foreign way of life that sometimes involved idolatry, a practice contrary to monotheistic Judaism.

The Lubavitcher Rebbe corresponded with many people on the subject of meditation, including several doctors. In one particular letter, dated January 1978 (Tevet, 5738), the Rebbe recognized the special healing capacities of TM and Yoga meditations, but tactfully expressed concern about some of their associated rituals that differ from those of Judaism. In the letter, the Rebbe states:

> *"Certain aspects of the said movements which are entirely irrelevant to religious worship or practices, have a therapeutic value, particularly in the area of relieving mental stress. It follows that if these therapeutic methods in so far as they are utterly devoid of any ritual implications would be adopted by doctors specializing in the field of mental illness, it would have a salutary effect*[40]*."*

Thus, the Lubavitcher Rebbe, as well as several other rabbis, encouraged the medical profession to open up to the field of meditation. As well, he advocated the establishment of Meditation centers that would employ the very same meditation techniques without the religious practices and rituals.

Since that time, the science of psychotherapy has welcomed meditation into its discipline, making it a mainstream therapy in Western countries. Today, even health insurance providers pay for these services.

Meditation, like psychotherapy, offers solutions to pain and suffering. In association with psychotherapy, meditation helps those who suffer from psychiatric symptoms or stress-related illnesses such as anxiety, tension or hypertension. According to psychiatrist Harold Bloomfield, a psychiatric patient necessitates *"only encouragement to meditate regularly and to engage in dynamic activity[41]"*. He quotes TM master Maharishi Mahesh Yogi, who states that the role of a psychotherapist towards a psychiatric patient who meditates is one of *"holding the patient's hand while TM does the healing[42]"*.

Meditation also has many physical benefits. It has been found to relax the body, lower cholesterol levels, reduce the intensity of pain and lower blood pressure. It can lower the heart rate, slow the breathing, and help overcome cravings for nicotine, alcohol and other drugs. Meditation is an effective form of healing for both physical and psychological conditions as it attaches us to our spiritual source and helps to draw down spiritual healing energies.

For all these reasons, meditation is being practiced by increasing numbers of people in America and around the world. However, the modern practice of meditation is often disassociated from its spiritual intent - the original raison d'être of meditation: the discovery of the soul as a truly infinite part of G-d.

Notwithstanding the professional separation of meditation from its spiritual roots, it appears that more and more people are seeking a higher truth. Today, the search for spirituality and G-dliness may be a compelling reason for many to turn to meditation.

Over the past few years, many popular entertainers such as Madonna and Michael Jackson have been said to have explored the ancient teachings of the Kabbalah and Jewish mysticism. The rising popularity of Jewish meditation is due to its complex and mystical nature as well as its close association with the Divine and its inclusion of both the emotional and the physical on the journey to spiritual enlightenment.

Jewish meditation is generating much interest simply because of what it uniquely offers: spiritual empowerment through the unification of the body and mind with G-d.

That something is lacking or amiss is a sign that you have found your mission, as that which is outwardly negative always conceals a goodness waiting to be uncovered. When you view a deficiency only as negative or repulsive, know that you yourself need healing, as you can only see a fault in another when you own that fault yourself. For this reason the Sages emphasized that we should not judge another until we have experienced his or her situation!

Chapter 7
The Benefits of Meditation

Abraham had a unique ability to concentrate on whatever he was doing, and to do so with the intent of drawing Divine energy into his being. Meditation is the exercise of removing thoughts that dominate our minds; it allows us to focus all of our mental energies upon a single thought or object. With the mind silenced and emptied of useless thoughts, it is liberated from its persistent and disruptive mental chatter. Judaism adds to the intellectual menu of meditation the involvement of the physical and emotional, enabling us to have Kavanah (Divine intention). With Kavanah, the mental tool that allows us to perceive purpose in everything we do, say or think, we elicit Divine force into our lives.

The Baal Shem Tov, founder of Chassidism, gave the following analogy: Far beneath the surface of the earth, G-d concealed many treasures. Although we all can dig for these treasures, when they are eventually found, we still must cleanse them from the Earth's impurities.

Think for a moment of a raw material such as a diamond. To convert it into a refined and useful product, we must first remove all layers of dirt and impurities. As long as external layers of dirt cover the diamond, we are unable to appreciate its true beauty. First, we must refine and polish it and then, finally, shape it into a beautiful and precious gem.

Man's natural unfocused state of mind can be compared to soil and earth. The clear serene mind that emerges through meditation can be compared to a hidden treasure.

If the mind is submerged in random thoughts, we can never really appreciate the secrets it holds. Meditation is a means through which we become more aware of the powers hidden within our souls; it brings us one step closer to awareness of our true selves.

The powers and benefits of meditation are limitless. By teaching us how to attain mastery of our thought processes, meditation brings us ever closer to emotional bliss.

During the 1960s and 1970s, physiologists worked on identifying the effects of meditation on the human mind and psyche. According to the studies conducted, during meditation a person reaches a relaxed state similar to certain stages of sleep, only the mind remains aware and thoughtful. Psychologist R.K. Wallace writes that a meditating person enters a special kind of physiological state, distinguishable from both sleep and wakefulness[43].

During meditation, the heart rate is much slower than during sleep, while oxygen intake is reduced. Researchers found that "alpha waves" are more apparent during meditation, particularly in the frontal and central areas of the brain[44]. These waves can also be followed by spontaneous showings of "theta waves".

Although psychological experiences are neither as tangible nor as measurable as physiological experiences, meditation has been shown to have significant benefits for mental and emotional states of being.

Meditation has been found to enhance visual acuity, auditory discrimination and the ability to concentrate. It also improves the synchronization between the right and left hemispheres of the brain, resulting in greater creativity, memorization and problem solving skills.

People who begin meditating report that it helps them to reduce fatigue, headaches, anxiety, and insomnia. In turn, these effects improve the quality of their social interaction at school and work[45].

The Kabbalah teaches us that emotions are deeply connected to the thought process. People often react without thinking first. A person who often erupts in anger is an example of one who behaves without clarity of mind. Such a person is oblivious to the consequences of actions motivated by anger, jealousy or pride. By practicing meditation, we can learn to avoid such situations and thus cleanse ourselves of such negative character traits.

Rabbi Schneur Zalman taught, *"The mind should influence the emotions of the heart"*. This is obviously not an easy task. Sometimes, it seems as if we've been pre-programmed to react with certain built-in emotions.

When one meditates, negative feelings can be calmed and then dissipated. At first it may be difficult to calm any negative emotions, but the more we practice meditation, the easier and more natural it becomes.

In Tanya, Rabbi Schneur Zalman explains that all human activities are animated by physical and spiritual tendencies he refers to as the "Divine Soul" and "Animalistic Soul". These two disparate souls, states Rabbi Schneur Zalman, are the source of the constant opposing viewpoints in man's never-ending inner struggle. The Animal Soul is the source of our character traits and natural human tendencies, yet without it, the Divine Soul could not express itself in our material world. The Divine Soul's selfless nature is to serve G-d and bond with Him. It also tries to influence the Animal Soul within and fill it with serenity and holiness. Although Jewish meditation encourages the sublimation of the Animal Soul to the Divine, it does not entirely exclude it from the journey toward spiritual development.

During prayer, it is the Divine Soul found within each and every person that speaks to G-d. It is this Divine Soul – a true spark of G-d – that puts man above all of creation. Ultimately, the Animal Soul is affected and joins the Divine Soul in the service of G-d. Initially, it will be against the will of the Animal Soul, but eventually it too is trained to do good deeds and act in conjunction with the Divine Soul.

Meditation is a tool that helps us reach true spiritual enlightenment by teaching us how to unite the intellect with the physical and the Animal Soul with the Divine Soul in the service of G-d. With the Animal Soul vitalizing the Divine Soul rather than opposing it, and the physical enhancing the realm of the intellectual, we can more easily reach an unsurpassed clarity of mind and experience the true inner divinity unaffected by the roughness life has layered over it. To experience the soul untouched by a lot of disturbing thoughts and emotions is to feel the breath of life in its purest form.

Yet, despite the spiritual, physical and intellectual benefits of meditation, it is no easy task to focus the mind. The mind naturally moves around like an animal in a field that demands its space. It seems that no matter what we are concentrating on, thoughts go through our minds at almost the same pace as commercial advertisements aired during a prime-time show on television. Meditation filters out all those disruptive mental commercials.

Imagine how much more pleasant it would be to watch a favorite show without the disruptions of commercials. It is easy to understand how meditation, which gives us such a focus, allows us more time and energy to do other things.

The mind functions like an ongoing film with flashes of thoughts and images coming from everywhere. It seems that sometimes we are its captive audience, prisoners of our own thoughts. It would be wonderful if we could shut off our thinking process at our whim.

By clearing our minds, we gain mastery over our power of thought. Thoughts that normally cause disturbance cease to be a nuisance. With the newfound clarity and freedom of mind afforded by meditation, we gain a greater capacity to confront the challenges that we address daily.

There are many meditative schools that teach methods of escaping the physical realm rather than remaining in the body to face our challenges. In Jewish meditation, the opposite is true.

The bedrock of Jewish meditation is to always draw down spirituality into the world, through our thoughts, speech and actions. This idea rests on the notion that when G-d created the world, He did so with the desire that He dwell within it.

Unique in its approach, Jewish meditation does not separate us from the mundane, but rather guides us through it into becoming more alert, mindful, clear-sighted and competent human beings. It allows us to develop and perfect our sensory organs and super-sensory processes. Eventually, by spending quality time working on ourselves, equilibrium is established within us whereby our thoughts and emotions are united.

We are able to express our emotions with greater sensitivity. Our speech is thought-out and results in actions that are similarly thought out. Our reflexes and reactions to challenges and frustrations become sharper and quicker.

Chassidism teaches that every action is influenced by our spoken word, which in turn is influenced by our thoughts. Whether the thought is positive or negative, its subsequent action will impact upon both the physical and spiritual realms. Thus, by acting on a positive thought, we draw positive energy down into the world. By acting on a negative thought, we draw negative energy down into the world. Through meditation, we are better able to choose and control the mark we will leave on the world.

Abraham taught all people that there is only one G-d. He understood that there is a unifying, all-encompassing existence that transcends and sustains all others. As Abraham was, we are commanded to "Go to You". We must find the oneness implicit within our mind, body and soul.

Chapter 8
Practices of Meditation

The very basic nature of meditation dictates that we seek to be at one with ourselves in mind, body and soul and at one with the world at large. This is made possible by developing our sense of awareness. Abraham saw this quality of oneness as the most important aspect in our relationship with G-d and all of mankind.

Many believe that the Torah (Bible) is the oldest scripture and most ancient source of wisdom still studied today. As such, it would be beneficial to examine the concept of awareness from a Torah perspective.

According to Torah, awareness elevates us in three ways. Firstly, through awareness, we gain insight into our own existence and relationship with our G-dly nature. Secondly, awareness gives us knowledge of our own mind, body and soul. Thirdly, the knowledge and insight garnered through awareness empowers us to transform our surroundings into a peaceful and spiritual dwelling place.

Several Eastern philosophies, Yoga, Buddhism and Zen included, have similar concepts of awareness as those found in the Torah. These Eastern faiths share with Judaism the goals of encouraging awareness of the self, the essence of the soul and the essence of the world. Since they were born of high-minded people who believed that life without spirituality is meaningless and unfulfilling, the conceptual core of these Eastern faiths is related to the pillars of Jewish faith and spirituality. Still, some of the philosophies discussed have been implemented in a way that sharply differentiates them from some of Judaism's most important tenets. My examination of the differences between Judaism and other faiths is not intended to cause division. On the contrary, I will show that while we practice differently, we are still all united through our common forefather Abraham. I want this book to increase respect and appreciation of diversity.

In the following chapters, I will discuss various Eastern philosophies, as well as Sufism and Christianity, so that the gifts of Abraham become clear. The words used to describe Eastern meditations and the Hebrew words used to describe that of the Torah's are often similar in meaning. However, the way the Eastern terms are spelled in Hebrew sometimes creates misspelled Hebrew words. Torah Sages explain that these words have been spelled in Hebrew with slight variations in order to distinguish them from their Torah counterparts.

The theory that Eastern religious wisdom and teachings were Abraham's legacy, a gift from the father of many religions, is evidenced by the striking similarities discussed in the following pages.

The master of Chassidic philosophy, the Baal Shem Tov, made it clear: There could only be the following directions. "That all is G-d, and G-d is all." At the point where these directions meet, there you will greet the Almighty.

Chapter 9
Hinduism

Abraham sent his children to India with gifts of spirituality, optimistic that they would use them to become acquainted with the One Creator G-d he had come to know. He shared with his sons the deepest secrets to ensure the growth and protection of their souls. Hinduism is a religion based on the nurturance of the soul. However, in Hinduism, the means used to arrive at this end are often antithetical to monotheism. Indeed, India's panoply of deities and their portrayal through images and statues opposes the Torah's perception of G-d, who is without shape or form. In Hinduism, one nurtures his or her soul by bonding with the many gods depicted in Hindu Scripture. In the Torah, however, the sources of life and vitality emanate only from the One Creator G-d.

Hinduism was influenced by many different religions. It is founded on the deification of nature and the worship of "Brahman", who is believed to be the essence and source of vitality for the universe. Unlike most religions, which practice a singular convention, Hinduism blends many diverse traditions, practices and beliefs. Aside from universal gods, Hinduism recognizes deities particular to certain cities, towns and communities in India.

Hindu scriptures are generally covered in four books Rig, Yajur, Sama and Atharva, known as the "Vedas", which in Indian means "the knowledge". These writings consist of lyrical hymns, prayers, praises of beauty and nature, rituals and practices.

One concept common to all of Hindu practice is the belief that all Divine revelations and emanations derive from Brahman. Brahman is said to be the ultimate unifier of all deities, and the sole possessor of the knowledge of how spiritual manifestations are drawn down into the world.

Akin to Catholicism's Trinity of Father, Son and Holy Spirit, Brahman is the culmination of three divinities: Brahma - the creator of the universe, Vishnu – the guardian of creation, and Shiva – the one who mandates movement and change.

Hinduism views the physical world as "Maya" - an illusion caused by our inability to see the true nature of reality. Even the physical self is considered an illusion. The Torah has a similar concept called "Olam Hasheker" - (the false world). Hinduism teaches that meditation is a method of escaping these illusions and connecting with the Brahman, usually described as the "world soul". The Torah sees meditation as a means for the soul to become more connected with the physical world.

It is interesting to note that the name "Brahman", in Hebrew and English, is similar to "Abraham". Brahman is also often referred to as "Sabda" Brahman. In Hebrew, Sabba is the word for grandfather. Thus in Hebrew, Sabda Brahman is strikingly similar to "Grandfather Abraham" or "Our forefather Abraham". There is also a striking resemblance between the interpretations of Brahman's traits and the qualities of Abraham.

The Hindu belief that Brahma and Brahman are the source of the drawing down of Divine emanations is similar to the Jewish concept of "hamshacha milema'alah lemata", the drawing down of G-dly sustenance from above. While describing the basic differences between Abraham and Isaac in his book <u>Torah Or</u>[46], Rabbi Schneur Zalman explains that Abraham's task was to cause a drawing forth of G-dliness from above to below. In <u>Tanya</u>[47], Rabbi Schneur Zalman also compares Abraham's connection to Divinity with water, whose nature it is to descend from a higher plane to a lower one.

According to Hindu beliefs, one must escape from the world's illusion to reach spiritual enlightenment. In Judaism, being grounded and navigating in worldly activity is a reality and a central theme. Thus, rather than avoiding situations which only hinder the attainment of spirituality, the Torah

Hinduism

teaches transforming these hindrances into positive accomplishments.

As mentioned in Chapter 3 of this book, Abraham pursued the task of making G-d known throughout the world. Sharing this great knowledge even with those who worshipped deities other than G-d, he influenced every person he came into contact with to recognize and pray to E-l Olam, the Eternal One, thus making G-d more revealed in this world[48]. Had Abraham considered the world as something from which he must escape, he would not have possessed nor fulfilled his mission of making G-d known and of drawing down spirituality for the benefit of mankind. He would also not have spent so much time bonding with people from all walks of life.

The very name of the Hindu writings, Vedas, also means knowledge in Hebrew. The Hindu Vedas, akin to Judaism's Torah, are considered to be the source of the wisdom that brings one closer to the Divine through every individual's self or soul - (Atman). In fact, the four books of the Vedas consist mostly of chants, prayers and hymns.

Moreover, the word Vedas is also similar to the Hebrew word for the service of the heart: "Avoda". On the verse *"And to serve him with all your hearts"*, Jewish Sages explain that the service of the heart is prayer. Both the Vedas and Avoda are replete with prayers, hymns and chants.

The Vedic scriptures discuss five levels of Creation. These five levels are strikingly similar to the five spiritual realms connected to the creation of the world as discussed in the Kabbalah. These realms are known as, "Adam Kadmon"- the Primordial Man; "Atzilut"- World of Emanation; "Beriyah"- World of Creation; "Yetzirah" - World of Formation; and "Asiyah" - World of Action.

The five levels of creation covered in the Vedic scriptures are:

"Purusa"- "The cosmic man" - of whose body the many parts of the universe are formed.

This is similar to what is known in the Kabbalah as "Adam Kadmon" - the most pristine emanation.

"Garbha" - The cosmic embryo or egg, which contains the totality of creation prior to any creative differences. This is akin to "Atzilut" since, at this level, only Divine light exists, removed from any form of existence.

"Creation"- At this stage, it is believed that a spiritual force called the "Creator" sheds His eternal light upon three realms, "heaven", "midregions" and "earth". This level, being the first of existence, is likened to "Beriyah" (Creation). At this stage, spirituality is contracted into spiritual vessels drawing vitality from the realm of "Atzilut". "Heaven" then provides vitality to the next two levels, the "midregions" and the "earth".

"Ambhas" / *"Salila"* - This realm, associated with water, acts as the primordial matrix of creation. It is associated to "Vac", the master of speech, in much the same way that Yetzirah is associated with speech and expression. Since water causes things to grow or emerge, this force causes the manifestation of things previously concealed, also characteristic of "Yetzirah".

"Tad Ekam"- meaning "the one and only", is the ultimate source of creation of the earth. The words "Tad Ekam" are comparable to the Hebrew words "Ehad Elokim", which mean the One G-d. In fact, according to the teachings of the Kabbalah, the physical world was indeed created by the Divine name "Elokim" whose numerical value in Hebrew is equal to the Hebrew word "Teva", for "nature ." This is similar to "Asiyah" at which point the four categories of life discussed above culminate and come to be in a physical way. Both According to

the Torah (Genesis ch. 1, verse 2), heaven and earth were created through the divine name *"Elokim"*.

Most Eastern traditions explain the process of creation in similar terms, stating that various agents and creative principles joined forces to bring forth the universe. However, in the Torah, G-d is depicted as the only master and controller of all levels of creation.

Hinduism also places a special emphasis on devotion. "Bhakti" is a service of contemplation and meditation on the Divine, culminating with the person meditating reaching ecstasy upon entry to the level of Brahman. In Hebrew, the word used to depict devotional service is "dbekut". The Hindu word bhakti, when spelled in Hebrew, uses the very same characters as the word dbekut.

A devout Hindu meditates three times daily (Sadhanas), at dawn, dusk and at noontime. This is similar to Judaism's practice of praying three times a day - Schacharit, Mincha and Maariv.

The country India is known in Hebrew as "Hodu". Hodu means to praise and glorify and is used often in the book of Psalms in its verses of thanks to G-d. The name Hodu may have come from the early settlers, notably the sons of Abraham sent off to the East who, according to the Midrash, praised and played musical instruments to various deities.

Hinduism generally consists of a five-tier belief system: Brahman himself, ancestors, various gods, spirits and human beings. Often, Hindus will use animal signs in order to depict certain godly energies. For example, the cow is a sacred symbol to all Hindus, as it represents the Divine energy nourishing all creation. The elephant god represents the power to subdue all turbulence and trials. The monkey god is the symbol of selflessness and spiritual ingenuity. While meditating, Hindu devotees will use these symbols as focus points. Such focus on these gods is incompatible with monotheistic belief and contrary to the Torah. In Judaism, devotion is directed only to G-d, Creator of the Universe.

Awareness of G-d must become an integral part of our life. Comprehending G-d is not only dependent on understanding the masters and teachers. Instead, it must come from our own insight and experience. In this way, we will find the reality of G-dliness in every part of our life.

Chapter 10
Buddhism

Abraham meditated to reach great unity with G-d. Particularly, while meditating he was able to go beyond his physical self and touch the essence of his soul. These were among the most precious gifts he gave to his children. Of all Eastern religions, Buddhism is probably the one most closely connected with spiritual meditation. Similar to that of the Torah's meditation, the goal of Buddhist meditation is to attain a state of mental freedom where the soul is awakened to the exquisite joy of worship.

The founder of Buddhism, Siddhartha Gautama, who lived during the sixth century BC, is said to have discovered enlightenment while meditating under the Bo tree at Bodh Gaya in Eastern India. According to Buddhist mythology, he sat under the tree for many days in solitude until he attained ecstasy. Due to his experience of enlightenment, he became known as the "Buddha" – the awakened one. He named his awareness "Nirvana" and proclaimed it the cure for all those who suffered from ignorance.

After his passing, the Buddha was looked upon as a source of enlightenment and freedom from suffering. The Buddha statue is still used as an object of worship and as a focal point for initiating meditations, practices not permissible in the Jewish religion.

Buddhist philosophy is focused mainly on "subduing ignorance". The Buddha believed that he could save people from suffering through his teachings. He gathered his thoughts together in a doctrine he called the "Four Noble Truths", which he describes as illness, pain, failure and death. According to Buddha, ignorance is caused by materialism, mankind's hunger for power and desire. Only by changing one's life and avoiding the causes of ignorance can one reach deep understanding.

The Buddhist belief that all evil, suffering, and negative feelings are a result of one's own ignorance is different from the Torah's view, which places these in the context of Divine Providence from the One Creator G-d. Judaism sees suffering as a cleansing of the soul which furthers awakening and closeness to G-d. G-d allows us to suffer at times, in order to arouse our hidden strengths and abilities.

The Torah looks upon "the Four Noble Truths" as opportunities for man to convert darkness into light. The goal of any dark situation is to reach for a higher enlightenment and deeper connection with the Divine. Even the negative aspects of the world were created by G-d and must therefore also have meaning and purpose.

Although Buddhism consists of several sects, it can be divided into two general groups: the "Hinayana" (lesser vehicle) and the "Mahayana" (the greater vehicle).

The "Hinayana", prevalent in Southeast Asia and Sri Lanka, believes in only the one historical Buddha. The "Mahayana", found mostly in Tibet, China and Japan, recognizes many Buddhas, some of which are said to be celestial and have never been incarnated. The Hinayana trust in "Boddhisattva", a messianic figure who promises to return to earth to enlighten all of mankind through "Nirvana".

Buddhists believe in many gods - spiritual forces that maintain and control the functioning of the earth. For this reason, Buddhism does not teach that it is the unique G-d as depicted in the Torah who created the world from nothingness. Buddhists believe that the many gods were originally human beings who enjoyed good karma during their physical existences and thus merited becoming deities. According to Buddhist tradition, all the gods will return to earth one day since earth is the place of enlightenment.

One Buddhist god is the "Amitabha Buddha", a most-trusted celestial Buddha who represents infinite light. It is said that he dominates a paradise known as "pure land", which anyone can earn access to by worshipping him.

According to Buddhist philosophy, the self is an illusion, since it is the source of suffering. Furthermore, to categorize one's self is false, since any description only limits a person's identity. Since Buddhists believe that all humans are in fact potential deities, any characterizations ascribed to the divinities are considered as limiting as any character depictions of an individual.

Buddhist philosophy does not grant exclusivity to G-d the Creator. Rather, Buddhists believe that within man alone lies the essence of all knowledge and enlightenment. For this reason, Buddhists believe that their gods must return to earth one day, as only on earth are they capable of challenging their minds and experiencing enlightenment.

In Judaism, acquisition of Divine wisdom necessitates selflessness before the unique Creator G-d. This begins with humility, also referred to in Chassidic philosophy as "nothingness", since it implies absorbing oneself within the light of G-d. That is, by selflessly and humbly following the guidelines of G-d's wisdom as embodied within the Torah, a higher meaning is given to the entities of this world.

In Hebrew, "nothingness" is described with the word "AYIN". When rearranging the letters of this word, one can obtain the word ANI, meaning "I"- as in the verse *"I am the L-rd, your G-d (Elokim)"*. Chassidic philosophy teaches that the Divine name Elokim also means "your strength and vitality". Thus, this verse implies that through one uniting with Him, G-d becomes the obvious source of energy in one's life. Consequently, in Judaism, at the highest level of nothingness a person becomes one - totally united with the Creator G-d.

Beyond the letter permutation argument, the conceptual similarity of "nothingness" - (AYIN) and Divine "everythingness" - (ANI, or I – which also represents the core of the individual universe) - is reiterated in the following morning prayer verse:

"You are the first and You are the last, and aside from You there is no (Ayin) G-d (Elokim). You were the same before the world was created. You were the same since the world has been created. You are the same in this world. And you are the same in the world to come[49]."

The word "nothing" or AYIN can be used to describe Elokim, the G-dly essence permeating all existence only because, according to Judaism, G-d's nothingness implies that all life is but a manifestation of His being. Hence, to become fully enlightened, prayer and meditation must be approached with the humility engendered by the quality of "nothingness" ascribed to both G-d and His human creations rather than with the egocentric "I" or ANI, which precludes the inherent source and unity of all life. Only with a humble mind freed of egoism and the limitations of human vocabulary can we move beyond the contradictions (everything, yet nothing – stagnant, yet ever changing) that define G-dliness, His creations (humanity) and our relationship with Him.

According to Rabbi Schneur Zalman's teachings on meditation[50], the mind contains three faculties that assist in the attainment of true enlightenment. They are chochma - (wisdom), bina - (knowledge) and da'at - (understanding). Together, they are referred to by their Hebrew acronym, Ch'aBaD.

Chochma - (wisdom) - is the first flash of intellect. It consists of two words in Hebrew, ko'ach[51] and mah[52], defined as "the potential of what is". It is the seminal point of an idea before it becomes clear or mentally comprehensible, the seed that contains all the hidden details of a potential idea in condensed form.

Chochma is also referred to as the "barak hamavrik" – the intuitive flash of G-d's enlightenment representing the first stage of intellectual discovery. In fact, it is said to be G-d's initial act of creation. The universe and everything in it was created through G-d's chochma. It is the intellectual faculty that represents G-d in all of creation.

Chochma is revealed through the faculty of bina - (knowledge) - which expands upon and elucidates the original intellectual point. With the faculty of bina, one contemplates and grapples with the acquired information, thereby crystallizing and clarifying all of its details until its essence is fully revealed.

Following the full knowledge of an idea, one finally reaches da'at - (understanding) - whereby the information acquired is integrated, becoming one with the person and part of his or her consciousness. At this level, comparable with Nirvana, one can be fully influenced by the idea at hand. This da'at is a culmination of the faculties of chochma - (wisdom) - and bina - (knowledge). Without da'at, an idea – (the offspring of bina and chochma) - remains abstract. Da'at influences the emotions and character, inspiring a person to physically act upon them.

Having the faculties of knowledge and understanding without the Divine wisdom of "chochma" is exemplified in a person who remains within his own mental capacity and does not seek to go beyond that level. As such, joining with G-d's infinity is difficult according to the Torah, since in our minds G-d is represented by chochma.

As mentioned earlier, the acronym for chochma, bina and da'at is ChaBaD. A central element in Chochma is the unique worship of the One G-d, Creator of the Universe. When the relationship with the Creator G-d is not absolute, the chochma can be separated from the ChaBaD combination. Thus, one is left with the Hebrew letters Bet and Dalet, which alone can spell "Bu ddha".

Life is about moving forward. Even when traveling to some specific destination, know that there is meaning to be found in the places where your feet temporarily stand.

Chapter 11
Zen Buddhism

From the moment he discovered G-d, Abraham devoted every moment of his life to disseminating the ethos and ideals of the Torah. Whoever he met and wherever he traveled, Abraham taught and practiced the importance of being focused both spiritually and physically.

Probably more than any other Eastern religion, Zen emphasizes the art of thinking in a controlled manner and directing the mind in a certain path. Although Zen's basic tenets differ from those of Judaism, there are some interesting similarities, as we shall soon see.

Meditation has a long history in the practice of Zen. In Japanese, the word Zen means meditation. It is said that Zen is a mixture of India's Mahayana Buddhism and Chinese Taoism.

The teachings of Zen are based on a wordless dissemination of wisdom. Zen preaches a form of enlightenment that is above and beyond any rational or logical conceptualization.

Zen philosophy is primarily based on a direct, speechless exchange of enlightenment between master and student. It is essentially a state of mind that seeks to look deeply into all aspects of life. It is the absorption of the mind into whatever one happens to be doing.

It is known that Zen's founder, Bodhidarma (AD 440-528), was a Buddhist from India. He conveyed his dedication to meditation with conclusive behavior. A prime example of this is his many-years-long meditation facing a rock wall.

Zen emphasizes emptiness of the self. By ridding the mind of most of its thoughts, an open space is made, allowing for the discovery of truth. According to Zen practitioners, it is within this emptiness of the thought process that one connects to the ultimate in enlightenment, the Buddha.

Zen doctrine is based on the Koans, a collection of paradoxes and stories about the interactions of Zen masters with their disciples. These stories convey the ideas and principles of Zen and are used by Zen followers as points of meditation.

Koan stories often include questions for which a clear answer will never be available. One well-known query asks: *"What is the sound of one hand clapping?"* Obviously, it must be silence, since clapping requires two hands. However, since silence is soundless, this cannot be the right answer.

The Koan stories cannot be understood with logic, since logic is contrary to Zen philosophy. The meanings and interpretation of Koan paradoxes are not found in the literal words or responses given. Rather, they are meant to develop the student's creativity and cognitive abilities while he or she searches for new insight.

Aside from using stories and paradoxes, Zen promotes contemplation and gazing. This is done with anything one comes into contact with or with any motion one makes. The goal is to learn to immerse one's mind in any activity, at any given time. Through such an immersion, the mind unites with the object or thing being contemplated. By virtue of immersion, Zen practitioners hope to experience unity of mind and body and find satiation through the soul.

This is similar to a classic Jewish teaching: *"Just as the Divinity permeates the world, the soul of man permeates the body. From the eyes of the soul, (the true awareness of one's being), a glimpse of things above can be attained"*.

It is interesting to note that the Zen concept of harmony of the mind and the physical self is similar to the teachings of the Kabbalah[53] on "Zun", meaning the union of the soul. In Hebrew, the word "Zun" would be spelled the same way as "Zen".

According to the Kabbalah, the Hebrew acronym Zun symbolizes the union of the six male - (Za) - and female - (Nukva) - emotive attributes. In turn, Zun serves as a bridge between the aspects of the soul most closely connected to the physical realm - (Nefesh) - and the world of action - (Asiyah). Since the higher spiritual levels of Atzilut - (the world of emanation), Briah - (the world of creation), and Yetzirah - (the world of formation) - all have their own particular forms of Zun, the Zun attained at the physical level actually derives from Atzilut, the highest level. At the lofty peak of Atzilut, Zun expresses the infinite, eternal light of G-d, offering access to and achievement of Divine understanding. However, even at the physical level of Nefesh - (the most tangible aspect of the soul) - Zun is beneficial for every human being, as it is essential in setting a balance within the mind and the soul domiciled within it. This concept of Zun in the Kabbalah is one of many that explain the connection between the Divine and the intellectual faculties of man, but also reinforces the role of both genders in spiritual development. It is interesting to note that for millennia Judaism has recognized gender equality and the need to balance female and male energies to develop emotionally and spiritually. Zun represents an ideal state of emotional stability, one in which balance is sought both within the mind and soul, and between a person's male and female spiritual traits.

By the time Zen reached Japan, it had already adopted practices that combined meditation with action. Zen in action is expressed through arts such as painting, calligraphy, poetry and the martial arts. Zen that combines the intellectual act of meditation with physical activity is known as "Zazen". Despite the phonetic similarity of Zazen – (or meditation in action) - with the Hebrew word "Zazin", which refers to the physical activity of the body, there are differences between Zen and Judaism.

According to Jewish thought, the soul possesses three powers that function as instruments of expression, namely thought, speech and action. Generally, they are referred to as the garments of the soul[54]. As it is with visible garments, these powers can be worn or removed at will. While the soul utilizes these garments, it is said to be "clothed" within them. When they are not used, it is divested of them. These garments also give expression to our minds and emotions in the same way that clothing portrays our individual status, function and style.

The goal of any Jewish meditative thought is to find its expression in action. Particularly, every meditation should be expressed by fulfilling the will of G-d as represented in the 613 mitzvoth - (decrees) - of the Torah.

The Torah teaches that we were created for the sole purpose of causing this physical world to become a spiritual dwelling place. To fulfill this mission, each person was entrusted with a Divine Soul. With our soul, we illuminate the world by adhering to the 613 Mitzvoth – Divine commandments.

The Zen concept of Zazen seeks to enhance and transform the mind's perception of the world. The Torah sees its Zun as an instrument that also transforms the world itself in a positive way. This type of meditation, which results in deep insight, is but the first step, according to Jewish philosophy – for it is confined to the intellectual realm of understanding or perspective.

Zen finds its origins in Buddhism, a religion that practices the near deification of Buddha and man. The Jewish monotheistic belief in the One Creator G-d as the only provider of life, vitality and energy for all entities is inconsistent with this ideology.

The recognition of the presence of a singular, all-encompassing G-dly force, capable of challenging and limiting the worthiest of man's efforts would seem to undermine some of Zen's notions of limitless freedom of mind. Judaism, however, sees G-d's revelation as the first step toward liberation. According to the Torah, one of the main characteristics of any mental imprisonment is the failure to see within this state a divine intent. Its nullification, explain the

Sages of the Torah, would be to find purpose within limitations and challenges. This can shake one out of self-absorption and expose one to spiritual awareness.

In Zen, awakening spirituality is best achieved with isolation from the physical world. Judaism, however, encourages using one's energy to make the physical world a fitting dwelling place for G-d's presence, since the Divine presence yearns to be revealed within the physical realm. In this sense, the Torah is often regarded as a map for changing the world and making it a habitation where G-d's presence is felt. In Judaism, to remove one's self from this world or to live within it as if it was an illusion is contrary to this notion. As mentioned in our chapter on Hinduism, Jewish Sages did often refer to this world as "olam hasheker" - the false world. However, it was called the false world only in the sense that it hides the true essence of G-d. Never is it prescribed that its existence or relevance should be denied. The Hebrew word for "world" is "olam", from the same root word as "helem", which means hidden. This signifies that everyone has the ability to undo layers of concealment within the world and reveal Divinity.

Remember that we are all agents of the One Above. There is only one G-d and this world is His dwelling. He has set His mandate in a manual called "Torah". G-d gives us the energy to represent Him within this world. This indeed is a privilege we must not squander!

Chapter 12
Taoism

The Sages state that G-d tested Abraham ten times, each test ending with a witnessed miracle. Still, it was not these miracles which brought him close to G-d. Rather, he realized that knowing G-d meant acquainting himself with G-d's natural world. He therefore spent much time in the mountains and in the wilderness, meditating for long hours in solitude.

Taoism, also known as Tao, is a Chinese philosophy that admires the power of nature. It dates back to the Gold Age of Chinese Philosophy - (500 – 221 BC). By the time Buddhism arrived in China from India, Tao had already become an important Chinese philosophy.

The founding of Tao is credited to two Chinese individuals Lao-Tzu and Chuang Tzu. Lao-Tzu taught by way of analogy, seeking to convey a sense of spirituality. His writings, although intriguing, are filled with ambiguities, lending his lessons an aura of mystery.

Many historians speculate that Lao-Tzu was a fictitious person created in order to convey lofty ideas and the possibility of supreme mental powers. Still, many stories are told about Lao-Tzu as a man who actually lived.

Tao's co-founder, Chuang Tzu, lived about 250 years after Lao-Tzu died. Unlike his predecessor, Chuang Tzu expressed his thoughts more clearly and logically with stories and fables.

According to legend, Lao-Tzu left China for India at a ripe old age and converted to Buddhism. Prior to leaving, he gave his followers his magnum opus, the "Tao Te Ching", and was never again seen in China.

A main feature of Taoism is that it seeks spirituality within nature. Like Buddhism, Hinduism and Zen, Taoism - a highly philosophical Eastern religion - has some things in common with Judaism.

The Tao emphasizes living life as naturally as possible. Tao, which in Chinese means the "nature of things", is based on the philosophy of accepting the natural order of the world and allowing nature to take its course. Human interaction can often interfere with attaining natural harmony and peace within the self. Thus, Taoists believe that perfection may be reached by simply resisting being impressed.

This Tao ideology is called "Wu Wei", meaning non-action. Tao non-action does not mean abstaining from any physical involvement or action. Rather, it implies allowing things to develop and grow naturally in their most authentic forms.

Wu Wei is founded on the idea that every cause has an effect and that everything is interrelated. Therefore, if one thing is negatively affected it will in turn have repercussions on a chain of related matters.

Taoists believe that seeking dominion over others and confronting evil can eventually lead to "good" being defeated. Consequently, the Tao advocates withholding any interference in the natural outcome of any given situation and allowing things to emerge as a matter of course. If the natural order of the world calls for one side to overcome and subdue the other, then that is best. The Torah's view on influence, however, is to always attempt to win over negative forces in order for good to prevail.

Chassidism teaches that a bad thing is only externally negative. Internally, even evil is good, only it is concealed with many layers. (For further discussion on evil, pain and suffering, please see chapter 20.)

When faced with a challenging situation, there are generally two options available: either to surrender to the circumstances or to try to transform the negative situation to one's benefit – i.e. subdue the darkness and convert it into light. According to Judaism, choosing to transform darkness awakens the higher powers normally dormant within one's soul. Thus in

Judaism, the purpose of any negative situation is to arouse one's deepest strengths and abilities.

Moving beyond Tao's Wu Wei theory of causality, a popular Chassidic teaching explains that everything we do in this world has an effect on what happens in the spiritual realms above. On the statement of Jewish Sages[55], *"Know what is above you,"* the Maggid of Mezritch, successor of the Baal Shem Tov, interprets: *"Know that everything above – all that exists within the spiritual realms – is from you – conditional on what you do within the physical world"*. Thus, every person has the potential to positively affect the highest levels of spirituality.

In fact, we influence our surroundings on a daily basis. For every word we speak, every thought we have and every action we take, there is a reaction. People in the world at large will react and reciprocate with positive qualities when we touch them with kindness or spirituality. This approach, in turn, also encourages an analogous response from Above.

The Tao teaches that everything has its opposite and both are necessary in order for mankind to develop. This is known as the "Yin and Yang" doctrine. For example, day exists because of night, the higher manifests itself in relation to the lower, redemption follows exile and death exists in comparison to life.

There is a similar doctrine in Jewish thought known as "zeh leumat zeh" - meaning that every positive entity has its counterpart, often in the realm of negativity. According to Kabbalah, the difference between the positive and the negative is that while the former receives its nourishment from holiness, the latter feeds off of the sources of darkness. Yet, even the sources of darkness acquire their vitality from holiness, although the holiness of that source remains concealed. In Tanya[56], Rabbi Schneur Zalman explains that everything in the realm of holiness has its counterpart in the kelipot, the negative shells that feed off of it.

Taoism

According to <u>Tanya</u>, our spiritual and physical tendencies are symbolized by two souls, referred to as the Animal Soul and the G-dly soul. The Animal Soul embodies faculties and garments - (thoughts, speech and action) - equivalent to those of the Divine Soul.

In Judaism, every entity possesses "Yin and Yang" - positive and negative features. Generally, while our Animal Soul is concerned only with its own needs, our G-dly soul - a pure manifestation of G-d - encourages the expression of its Divine nature and seeks to convey the G-dliness embodied within the world.

Taoists view the world as existing naturally. That is, man is to accept events "as is" without seeking to influence them. To understand that opposites function separately and independently leads to enlightenment. According to Taoism, the manifold divisions existing within the world must be kept intact by keeping them separate, since each entity has its own uniqueness. Man may see himself as one of the many entities of this universe, but not as a being that has the duty to mold material existence and elevate the world. Taoists believe that the mind can only experience true freedom and spirit if the independence of all elements is preserved.

The Torah Sages see man, the universe and the Divine as a complete, interdependent unity embodied in a relationship based on give and take. It is therefore incumbent upon us all to establish a sense of peace between our physical self and our higher spiritual being. This entails seeing both the body and Animal Soul as vehicles carrying the Will of the Divine Soul throughout one's life. Necessarily, we must see ourselves as capable of influencing our environment and subduing negativity and evil.

Having been gifted with an intelligent and Divine soul, each person is obliged to bring creation to its ultimate destiny. One can only fulfill one's duty by interacting with the environment and the people within it; and then by spiritually transforming and elevating one's surroundings to correlate with the world. In this way, one is empowered to accomplish the purpose of one's own creation – making a dwelling - (bayit) - for G-dliness within the physical realm.

Taoism's name for the inner energy latent within all entities is "chi" – the breath of life. Taoists believe that every entity in nature owes its survival to chi, the force that vivifies all elements with life and energy. Interestingly, if spelled in Hebrew, the word "chi" would read as "chai", which also refers to the life force and vitality implicit within every living entity. Judaism believes that this chai breath of life comes directly from our Creator G-d[57].

The very word "Tao" and its definition are analogous with the Hebrew word "teva", which also refers to the nature of things. Interestingly, Tao in Hebrew can be spelled with the same letters as teva, by removing the middle letter Bet. On a deeper level, the letters that constitute the word "teva" in Hebrew are numerically equivalent to the Divine name "Elokim", which refers to G-d as He provides energy within all physical entities.

According to the Kabbalah, G-d has many names that He uses to draw His Divine energy into the world. For example, there is a supreme energy that comes from a level above Elokim, known as "Havayah". Above this level, there is that of "Atah" or "Anochi", which represents the essence of the Divine. For our purposes, it is important to understand that the infinite energy embodied within Elokim – (teva) - goes through a process called "tzimtzum" – (concealment and contraction of G-dly light and life force). In this way, nature is created and sustained.

This process of "tzimtzum" involves a series of emanations necessary in order for the material to retain its physicality while receiving this spiritual light. Like a chain composed of many rings, successive levels of G-dliness move from the infinite to the finite.

At each level, less light and life force is radiated so that the lower beings can survive and not lose their identities. Too much spiritual light would cause the recipient to be nullified from existence.

The name "Elokim" which is written in the plural form, suggests that every entity receives its own unique and separate life force. According to the Torah, G-d chose to create the universe with the Divine name "Elokim" in order to reflect diversity and the many natural divisions that exist within our world. Each level of creation acquires light pursuant to the limits of its physical vessel. Thus, according to Judaism, the prime mover of nature is Elokim[58].

Akin to Taoist philosophy, Judaism views man as being born into a world of concealment - (Maya). Like plants that grow in a field, people tend to grow independently of each other. Although independence can be a means to arrive at completion and purity, still the quest for spirituality cannot end there. According to Judaism, the soul reaches full development after binding with others and uniting with G-d, our Creator.

Taoists believe that immortality follows the realization of one's full potential, both physically and spiritually. By growing independently of and unaffected by the environment, man can actually live for centuries within the same physical body. Judaism, on the other hand, also greatly emphasizes personal development, but as a by-product of interrelationship and co-relationship with the environment. This relationship is crucial for our personal growth and necessary to fulfill our Divine mission to make the world a dwelling place for G-d. Thus, all were given access to the Mitzvoth of the Torah to refine and transform the physical world into a more meaningful realm.

As mentioned earlier, the Hebrew word for nature – "Teva"- is comparable in meaning to the word "Tao". However, the Hebrew letter Bet is absent from "Tao". Interestingly, the letter Bet is also the Hebrew word for home or dwelling place. The Sages explain that the letter Bet is a constant reminder that every thought conceived, word spoken or action rendered helps to make the world into a home for G-d to dwell in.

In the mortal realm, physical intimacy is more than a unity between two bodies. It gives birth to new life. So too, a person's bond with G-d stimulates energy and creation. Don't be intimidated to fraternize with G-d!

Chapter 13
Yoga

Abraham did everything in his power to unite people with G-d in body, mind and soul. Every one of his meditations was followed by a positive physical act. Abraham not only taught people how to think spiritually, but also how to practice acts of kindness. In fact, the Kabbalah explains that his hospitality aroused more Divine energy than his spiritual service to G-d.

Yoga, an art which emphasizes unity of the mind and body, is a very popular form of physical exercise at aerobic centers and sporting clubs all over the Western world. Yoga can find its place in Judaism as a discipline for both a healthier mind and body, provided that its religious practices involving deities is avoided.

The philosophy of Yoga originally emerged in India and was very much influenced by Hinduism. It is a philosophy that places tremendous importance on both achieving a higher consciousness and maintaining a healthy physique. Its founder, Patanjali, sought to teach people how to create a peaceful, harmonious relationship between their physical and spiritual selves and maintain a balance between the intellect and the emotions. Patanjali organized his many Yoga practices into the "Yoga Aphorisms". These teachings seek to create a sense of harmony between the mind, the body and the universe. Through the practice of Yoga, one can arrive at the Hindu destination of an unchanging inner oneness within the universe.

Yoga philosophy teaches that every person has a soul - (Atman) - which, like in Judaism, is an expression of Divinity. Furthermore, Divinity expresses itself within the world as "Brahman".

The word "Yoga" in Sanskrit means to bond and to unify. Thus, within the name Yoga itself, the point of its philosophy is implicit. Since, by unifying the intellect with the body one connects to the source of energy, Yoga involves mental and physical exercises bent on maintaining both a healthy body and soul.

Many other meditative religions such as Zen, Buddhism, and Taoism have adopted Yoga methods of concentration and control. For example, controlled breathing plays a central role in Yoga's mastering of the body and mind.

In the philosophy of Yoga, learning to command one's heartbeat and body temperature is essential in building strength and mind control.

The Yoga Aphorisms are based on eight commandments, known as the eight limbs of Yoga. The first two are: "Yama" - the prohibitions against immoral actions such as killing, stealing etc., and "Niyama" - the positive commandments such as acts of kindness, of love, humility, health, etc.

The other six are "Asana", "Hatha", "Parayama", "Pratyahara", "Dhyana" and "Samadhi" which involve various Yoga exercises, breathing techniques, meditations and enlightenment practices.

The similarities between the eight principles of Yoga and the Ten Commandments that form the basis of the Torah are very obvious. However, there are a few very important distinctions between the Ten Commandments and the Yoga Aphorisms.

The first two commandments which form the bedrock of Jewish belief in G-d are: *"I am G-d the L-rd"* and *"Thou shall have no other gods (but Myself)"*. These first two Torah Commandments are absent in spirit from the Yoga Aphorisms, as Yoga practices involve devotion to many deities. Yet, Yoga's "Yama" and "Niyama" commandments are similar in principle with the other eight commandments of the Torah in that they have to do with upholding morals and ethics.

The word Yoga, when spelled in Hebrew, can also be pronounced as "yegia". Yegia means to strive and to reach –

ultimately to bond to and unite with the substance one is reaching for. As with the Mitzvoth, the eight Yoga Aphorisms seek to connect the body and soul with the universe. In Judaism however, the tremendous power of those first two commandments not included in Yoga provide a further unity by then bonding body, soul and universe to the unique Master of the universe, G-d, our Creator.

In Psalms 128:2, King David writes: *"If you strive (Yegia) physically... then you will be praiseworthy and you will prosper"*. The Sages explain that we can approach life in two different ways. Either our minds and souls toil with the body to face the challenges of our physical world or our minds and souls are protected, while our body alone struggles with our physical challenges. Authored by King David, the Psalms suggest that we can only prosper when the striving and toiling are restricted to our body – since only then are our minds and souls free to meditate and contemplate G-dliness.

Another teaching of the Sages states[59]: *"If I reached (Yagati) and I discovered, then (believe) me"*. According to this teaching, we must struggle spiritually in order to touch the Divine and bring it down into the physical world. Struggle is necessary in any successful effort to touch the Divine and draw it down, since without struggle, the barriers that stand between heaven and earth cannot be broken. To draw Divinity into the world, one must be prepared to devote one's self and one's material needs. Without devotion, attachment to G-d is always limited.

Thus, in Judaism, "Yegia" is a means of transforming and subjugating the body and the material world only until both become proper receptacles for G-dliness. Physical activities such as the performance of the Mitzvoth - (Divine commandments) – allows for discovering G-d in natural settings, rather than in supernatural realms. Every physical movement and striving must aim to make the world a dwelling place for G-d – igniting a light within the world, not above it.

Over the ages, many forms of Yoga have developed. The most popular, at least for the Western world, is Hatha Yoga. This technique consists of safeguarding a healthy body through exercises, healthy eating, high sanitary standards and body posture. Other techniques of Yoga focus more on mental exercises or physical development.

Due to the Yoga emphasis on health, practitioners of Buddhist, Zen, and Taoist meditation include Yoga techniques and philosophy in their practices.

Although the practice of Yoga is similar in certain ways to Judaism, its foundations are not based on monotheistic principles. Indeed, the cornerstone of Yoga and most other Hindu religions is the belief in various deities as expressions of the Divine. Hindus believe that all the gods combined together form one superior spiritual force that activates the Universe and allows things to exist. It is up to the Yogi to connect with not one, but many deities in order to reach a higher realm.

In accordance with these beliefs, "Atman", the soul of man, is an expression of these deities. Thus, Yoga's emphasis on reaching a higher state of consciousness and a healthier body is based on the realization that one's essence originates in various deities. It is thought that this awareness liberates man from his finite self. Meanwhile, Judaism teaches that the only true freedom one can experience results from tapping into one's soul and connecting with none other than G-d, the one and only Creator of the Universe.

Aharon's sons so hungered to touch the face of G-d that they escalated to the sublime light and there they died. Upon reaching the sublime light, their duty was to return to express G-dliness within physical life. They failed in this mission. Escape from the physical is only for rejuvenating the soul with fresh energy. The soul must then share this Divine light with others in the darker material world.

Chapter 14

Islam's Sufism

The Midrash says that four people were named by G-d before birth. Among them was Abraham's first born son Ishmael. The Sages explain his being named before birth implied that he had special potential to rise to greatness. For this reason, Abraham thought that perhaps the Torah would be given to the descendants of Ishmael. However, G-d revealed to him that his wife Sarah would bear a son named Isaac whose children were destined to receive the Torah on Mount Sinai. Nonetheless, Ishmael was blessed by Abraham to be the father of a fruitful nation and to possess great wealth. Ishmael's descendants, born to his Egyptian wife, were later known as the Ishmaelim, the biblical reference to the early Arabs.

Abraham prophesized that Ishmael would beget twelve princes who would form a great nation on the face of the earth. The descendants of Ishmael were Nebaith, Kedaar, Adbell, Mibsam Mishmah, Dumah, Hadad, Temah, Yetur, Nafish and Kedem. Indeed, from Abraham's blessings, the Arabic descendants of Ishmael became a great nation, particularly after the rise of Islam in 624 CE. In Islam, principle obligations for a faithful Muslim are, trust in *Allah*, reverence in Muhammad its founder, fasting and prayer. Many will also practice pilgrimage to Mecca where Muslims believe that Abraham had founded the famous House of Prayer. As well, it is a Muslim conviction that the sections which speak about G-d's Oneness in the Koran, "The Recital" or in Arabic *Qu'an*, taught by Muhammad, derive from Abraham's teachings on the subject. Muhammad born in A.D. 570 in Mecca, was the son of Abdullah bin Abd al-Muttalib of a tribe called Quarysh and of a woman named Aminah. Prior to his religious influence, many Arabs practiced paganism, perhaps since the time of Ishmael. Not only did the Meccans worship *Allah*, but also several female gods said to be the daughters of *Allah*. It is an accepted view that Muhammad's teachings on the exclusive devotion to the One G-d, was influenced by Judaism and of certain monotonous spiritual Arabs called *Hanifs*. According to Muslim tradition, it happened one evening in 610 CE, that Muhammad while meditating, had fallen into a trance and saw a vision that he must teach the way of Islam based on submission to *Allah*.

The Torah describes the Ishmaelim as desert people who settled throughout the Middle Eastern Region, from Syria to Yemen.

Abraham, who personally circumcised his son Ishmael, taught him about the power of meditative prayer. Indeed, throughout history, the descendants of Ishmael have always been known for their deep contemplative devotion towards the Al-mighty *Allah*. Although known as the mystical branch of Islam, Sufism emerged long after the 7th century era of Muhammad. Throughout its history, various masters have led the Sufist movement, each with his own distinct style. Thus, the practice of Sufism changed from century to century and from location to location. However, its principal ideals remained the same.

The path of the Sufi is a spiritual journey whereby from the act of separating from the body, one is drawn into a longing and ecstasy to be attached to G-d. The Sufi level of ecstasy is so intense that it is similar to the Hindu's "Bhakti" - the deep devotional service of the heart usually practiced to reach an altered state of mind and deep trance.

In his service to G-d, the Jew and the Sufi share a burning love and longing for attachment to G-d, but for the Jew, escape from the body is neither suggested nor necessary. According to the Torah, the Jewish path is one in which one relies on the body in the quest to make the world a better place, a proper dwelling place for G-dliness to be felt.

Sufi teachings are usually transmitted by way of stories and anecdotes. These stories are often told in a manner that does not convey immediate sense. They are expressed in this way in order to awaken within the listener a yearning to know the essential truth hidden within them.

One of the best-known Sufi stories is as follows:

> Once, a person was looking on the street for a key that he had lost. A passer-by noticed the person desperately looking for something and offered to help him. The passer-by asked: *"Where did you lose your key?"* *"I lost my key in my house"*, the person replied. The passer-by then asked: *"Why are you looking for it on the street and not in the house?"* The person responded: *"On the street there is more light."*

Sufi meditation is usually practiced by breathing rhythmically and chanting a biblical verse or meaningful words, quietly or out loud. This practice is called "ZIECHR" – (to remember) - alluding to the recollection of the Divine. The Arabic word "ZIECHR" is similar to the Hebrew word "ZECHOR", which also means "to remember".

In Judaism, remembering is considered to be a spiritual achievement when associated with important G-dly events of the past. On Esther 9:28: *"And these days shall be remembered and done"*, the Sages explain that when a special day or holiday is remembered within the physical realm below, the initial event is re-enacted within the spiritual realms above. This means that the Divine energy that existed at the time of the event is again reawakened by acts of recollection.

For this reason, Jews are to remember the liberation from the ancient Egyptian bondage, not only on Passover, but every day of the year. Going out of Egypt has additional spiritual significance when we view ourselves going out of our own personal "Egypt". Freedom from Egypt is the liberation of the soul from the obstructions of material life. In Hebrew, the word for Egypt, "Mitzrayim", also means limitations and constraints. In Psalms, chapter 118, verse 5, King David uses a derivative of the word "Mitzrayim" to describe his own desire to be freed from limitations. He writes: *"From out of narrowness I called upon G-d, with expansiveness free me."* If freedom of the soul is to be acquired, then fleeing one's personal limitations must be practiced regularly. We must constantly liberate ourselves from the obstacles and limitations we find ourselves surrounded with.

Sufis also practice "Dhikr" - total focus on the name of G-d, referred to in Arabic as *Allah*. By constantly repeating the name *Allah*, Sufis believe that G-d will descend upon them and draw them out of their bodies into a state of ecstasy. The goal is to come to a point where awareness of the physical self is completely lost. Dhikr is similar to the Hebrew word Dhakr – to convert and refine an object into a useful product. When referring to concepts and ideas, the word Dhikduk - (exactness or detail) - or Dhikdek - (to examine and to observe with care) - are used.

The Hebrew words Dhakr, Dhikduk and Dhikdek derive from the root word Dhak - (to scrutinize). Thus, when the meaning of these words is applied to the mind, they point to meditation as an instrument to become more aware of hidden soul powers. Man's natural state of mind is unfocused. When our minds are engaged by random thoughts, it is very difficult to appreciate its jewels. However, when our mind is cleared through meditation, its hidden treasures are revealed.

The most popular Sufi meditation in America is the spinning dance called "Mevlevi". In this dance, the left arm is lifted upward with the palm of the hand wide open as if to attach itself to the heavens. The right arm is oriented downward with the palm open in order to transmit energy below. The dancers spin on their heels and meditate on *Allah*. The goal of this dance is to reach an altered state of mind in which the dancer's soul is freed of the body.

In an important Kabbalah text called "Shoshan Sodot" – Rose of Mysteries[60] - Rabbi Moshe Ben Yaakov of Kiev describes three ways in which we can divest ourselves of our physical bodies: "the Kabbalah approach", "the philosophical approach" and "the common approach".

In explaining the "Kabbalah approach", the author refers to the practices of his master, Rabbi Abraham Abulafia, one of the most important Kabbalistic figures who lived during 13th century.

Rabbi Abulafia taught him the importance of erasing all useless thoughts from the mind and how to focus on methods of the Hebrew letter permutations – the interchanging and substituting letters that spell the various names of G-d. Rabbi Abulafia then revealed to the author the mystery of the normally incomprehensible Divine names, and advised him in "The Path of Names[61]". Rabbi Moshe spent two months meditating on these names until he awoke once in the middle of the night to see his face illuminated with great light. From then on, the light followed him wherever he went.

When his master Rabbi Abulafia heard of this great experience, he gave permission to his noble disciple to begin utilizing the Divine names practically. This eventually led to Rabbi Moshe's acquisition of a great elevation in holiness and the ability to speak fluently about the most secret aspects of mysticism.

With respect to the "philosophical approach", Rabbi Moshe refers to a philosopher named Ben Sina, who while in a state of intellectual meditation, shed light on esoteric wisdom in writing. In speaking of the "common approach", Rabbi Moshe describes a method known as "Mechikah[62]", the divesting or erasing all foreign matter from the mind. Through this kind of meditation any and all useless thoughts or even images can be obliterated from the mind.

Rabbi Moshe observed that the Muslim Sufis who repeat a chant concerning *Allah* are in fact practicing Mechikah, and could indeed reach a certain degree of ecstasy. The secret and powerful permutations of the Holy Names of G-d are found through interchanging and substituting Hebrew letters, as found in the Zohar. Rabbi Moshe explains that without this knowledge, it is much more difficult for one to truly unite with G-d.

As we mentioned, the name "Sufi" refers to the ecstatic attachment with the light of *Allah* (G-d). The name "Sufi" is similar in spelling and in meaning to the Hebrew word Sof as in the expression "Ein Sof[63]"- ("eternal light") - often used in the Kabbalah when referring to G-d's creation and sustenance of the world. The word "Ein" means "none other" and the word "Sof" denotes "eternal". Together it is translated as "The Eternal G-d". This is also demonstrated by the "I" of Sufi, which, in Hebrew, would be equivalent to the letter "Yud" - the first letter of the TETRAGAMATION, the "nomen proprium". The "Yud" - (I) - in Hebrew refers to the highest level of revelation and to "none other except for G-d". A Sufi mantra referring to this concept, "La Ilahah" - (to the One G-d) - is identical to the Hebrew words and meaning for this concept.

According to Chassidic philosophy, "Ein Sof" is also the strength and creative force of what is unholy, but at a much decreased level. While the holy receives its substance directly from "Ein Sof", the unholy is given indirect light from "behind the back" of "Ein Sof". Since the "kelipot" - (external forces) - do not see the face of Ein Sof, they imagine themselves as independent and separate from the Divine hand that sustains them.

The Baal Shem Tov taught that through devotional prayer and meditation, a very deep and close attachment to "Ein Sof" can be developed while remaining within the body. Conversely, Sufi Meditation is used to reach an altered state of mind whereby the soul is felt to be free from the constraints of the body.

In Judaism, the search for an altered state of mind is not a goal in and of itself, because the very purpose of the soul is to reside within a physical body. Souls are clothed within bodies so that the two work in tandem to draw spirituality into the world and elevate the sparks of holiness latent within all physical entities.

In Judaism, any highly spiritual experience has the purpose of energizing the person to serve G-d and do good deeds within the physical world. In the Kabbalah, this is referred to as "Ratzu and Shuv", or "advance and return" - a concept somewhat similar to transcendental meditation, known simply as TM. With "Ratzu and Shuv" it is possible to experience ecstasy to the point where the soul so yearns for a union with G-d that it is about to separate from the body[64]. At the moment of arrival at the highest point, one must return to the mundane world to continue serving G-d with rejuvenated spiritual bliss.

Rabbi Schneur Zalman describes Ratzu and Shuv as a two-pronged process of meditation and action[65]. Service to G-d must move beyond hearts and minds and be concretized into material consequences so that mystical union with G-d is completed.

According to Judaism, bodies and other physical materials are to be used as instruments to attach one to the Divine and make the environment a fitting place for G-d to reside. For example, parchment made from animal hides can be used to create holy articles such as a Sefer Torah - (handwritten scroll of the entire Torah), a Mezuzah - (mini handwritten scroll of select verses placed on the doorpost) or a pair of tefillin - (phylacteries worn during morning prayers also including handwritten scrolls). By inscribing the sacred words of the Torah on parchment, the animal, as well as everything used in preparation is elevated and one's spiritual and physical duties are fulfilled.

Although forbidden in Judaism, there are two reasons why one would want to divorce oneself completely from the physical realm. A person can feel such a profound yearning and love for G-d that the body can no longer contain the soul, leading to its detachment from the world. Or, one may find corporeality and the material so repugnant that the only desire remaining is to flee from the constraints of physical existence.

Any excuse or justification for the attempt to remove the soul from the body prevents one from living according to the Torah, which teaches that G-d intends the physical world He created to be filled with his Mitzvoth and not emptied. According to the Sages, total separation from physicality is equivalent to abandoning the fulfillment of one's role within Creation, as evidenced in the story of Aharon's two sons, Nadav and Avihu.

The Torah portion of "Acharei" (Leviticus, 16-1) begins with the words: *"G-d spoke to Moses after the death of Aharon's two sons, upon drawing close to G-d and they died."* Why does the verse conclude *"and they died"* when the Torah previously states *"after the death of Aharon's two sons"*?

The famous Sage Or Hachaim[66] explains their death as follows. Nadav and Avihu came close to a sublime light with holy love and died because of it. This is the mystical secret of "G-d's kiss" through which the righteous ones die. Their death was equivalent to the death of the righteous, but with a distinction. It is the kiss of G-d that approaches the righteous, while in this instance, it was they who approached it. Although they understood that they would die, they did not hold back from coming close and clinging to G-d in a sweet bond of love to the extent that their souls departed.

Chassidic philosophy explains that the love of G-d must involve the two phases mentioned above, notably "Ratzu and Shuv". While Ratzu is the deep yearning for attachment to G-d, Shuv is the commitment to return to the body and express G-d's will within the physical world.

Aharon's sons had reached a powerful level of Ratzu, and longed to be attached to G-d. Their sin was that their desire to reach the Divine was not followed by Shuv, and thus they died. Their attachment to G-d escalated to such intensity that their bodies could no longer embody their souls. This is implicit in the words of the Torah when it says, *"when they drew near to the L-rd (with such intense ardor that) they died."*

Their escape from the realities of the body was considered sinful, since, contrary to Divine intention, they moved beyond filling the environment with spirituality befitting G-d, thus moving beyond life itself.

This subject brings to mind the following question: If one is experiencing a genuine ecstasy or spiritual trance, can we truly expect him or her to let go of this sublime feeling and return to his or her physical limitations?

The answer to this question depends on the way that person initiated his or her spiritual journey. If the person set out to satisfy personal sublime desires, then he or she will have difficulty making the proper efforts to return from the personal ecstasy for the sake of physical life. If, on the other hand, the person sees submission to G-d's will as crucial, then he or she will return from the ecstasy to fill the world with spirituality and make it a dwelling place for His presence.

"Ratzu and Shuv" solidify the soul's attachment to the physical body and foster the drawing down into the world of the energies of any mystical experience achieved. According to Judaism, within the ecstatic approach to G-d, the desire to return and sanctify the world must always be at the forefront.

Redemption is freedom from the limitations that restrict the human spirit. It can occur by arousing our essential connection with G-d and with our fellow being. Throughout the ages, individuals like Moses our teacher who encouraged us to yearn for freedom. See that you were created in the image of G-d and that you were given the power to bring freedom. Tap into your soul and awaken your innermost resources!

Chapter 15
Christianity

Christianity, with its roots in Judaism, possesses several common themes with the Jewish religion. However, there are integral differences, as we shall describe.

The Torah alludes to Christianity when it speaks of the birth of Esau, Abraham's grandson. In the portion of Toldot, Chapter 25, verse 30, it states that he was also called Edom, a name used in reference to Christianity. Christianity is founded on the teachings of a young Jew named Yoshua of Nazareth, better known as Jesus. Initially a student of the famous Sage Rabbi Yehoshua Ben Perachya, he later attracted his own followers. Jewish sources provide little information about him.

It is known that the celebrated Sage Hillel lived just before him. One of the great teachings of Hillel, which probably influenced Jesus, was that of loving-kindness. In fact, Hillel used to say that loving your fellow as yourself is comparable to fulfilling the entire Torah.

During the early years of Jesus, one of the most revered Masters was his teacher Rabbi Yehosua Ben Perachya. Perhaps one of the most celebrated teachings of Rabbi Yehosua Ben Perachya was the following: *"Provide yourself with a Master, acquire for yourself a friend, and every person favorably (Ethics of our Fathers, Ch.1, Section 6)"*. The message is not simply to have any teacher, but also a guide who will know you and be there for you in times of need. However, the guidance of a Master is not enough without the presence of a close friend at your own level with whom you can share your challenges and trials. More interesting is his teaching about seeing the good intent in every person, no matter how wrong that person's actions may seem.

There is an interesting discussion recorded in the Talmud (Sanhedrin 107b) between Rabbi Yehoshua Ben Perachya and Jesus. The Talmud sets the background by stating that Jesus and his rabbi fled to Alexandria in Egypt because a certain King Yannai had killed many Torah scholars. One day, while Rabbi Yehoshua Ben Perachya was reciting the Shema prayer, Jesus walked into his presence. When his rabbi motioned to him with his hand that he needed to speak to him, Jesus thought that his rabbi was repelling him. He left the premises, but his rabbi called him back. They then began talking about repentance. Jesus reminded his rabbi of his previous strict rule that a person who sins and also causes others to sin is not given the opportunity to repent. Rabbi Yehoshua Ben Perachya then reminded him of another teaching that if a person makes a sincere effort to refine himself, G-d will understand and accept. Similarly, our own judgment of others needs an understanding heart, because of the challenges people encounter. The individual being challenged should know that G-d only places us in situations we can handle. The person judging must know that G-d provided the challenged individual with the necessary abilities to successfully overcome the challenge.

Immediately following the lifetime of Jesus lived the great Talmudic sage Rabbi Akivah who continued the path of wisdom of his predecessors. He taught among other things that everything G-d does He does for the good - the meaning of martyrdom and the signs of the promised Messiah. Rabbi Akivah saw it as his duty to teach the Torah to as many people as possible. He personally taught tens of thousands of students, many of which became great Kabbalah masters and Talmudic scholars. Like many of his peers, he also died as a martyr at the hands of the Romans. He was tortured to death in the presence of his students for the crime of teaching the Torah.

Christianity began to flourish a short time after Jesus died. Paul of Tarsus, who never met Jesus during his lifetime, disseminated Christianity as we know it today. Initially, Paul stood against the first supporters of Christianity, but then later himself became a Christian. Originally known as Saul, Paul to its ultimate purpose. Although we are limited beings, we still posses a Divine Soul connected to G-d. With this soul, we remain connected to G-d and feel the motivation to follow His will. The Torah and its Mitzvoth are the blueprint for accomplishing this goal. Yet, the Torah is not just a textbook. One must apply one's own mind and heart to serve G-d in the best possible way.

It is interesting to observe that the Hebrew word for agent - "shaliach" - hints to the fulfillment of man's mission. In the Hebrew language every letter has a numerical value. The numerical value of shaliach, along with the number ten, equals the name Messiah. Man's ultimate goal is to prepare the world for the Messiah. The Messiah will lead the world to a permanent era of peace, tranquility and unity. Chassidic teachings explain that each person making use of his or her ten soul powers hastens the Messiah's coming. (According to Kabbalah, the soul consists of ten faculties, each one an active contributing character trait to the soul. For further discussion, please see chapter 17 of this book.) Moreover, fulfilling the Ten Commandments elevates the world which, according to the Kabbalah, was created by ten utterances pronounced by G-d.

After more than two thousand years of exile and the recent dramatic changes on the world scene, Jewish leaders have maintained that the world is now poised for the imminent revelation of the promised Messiah. Adding in acts of goodness and kindness will greatly precipitate this era.

PART II

JEWISH MEDITATION

Jewish Meditation

As mentioned several times throughout this book, Abraham is the father of meditation. This is not to say that Adam, the first man, or his children did not meditate. On the contrary, the Sages tell us that Adam possessed infinite wisdom about esotericism and the deepest secrets of creation. The Sages of Kabbalah even tell us that Adam's wisdom about creation and mysticism was handed down to Abraham and probably influenced the writing of his Book on Creation, discussed previously. Nonetheless, Abraham, unlike his predecessors, was the historic rejuvenator of the idea of the one, unique, indivisible and indefinable G-d.

The Sages of the Midrash tell us that from Creation, G-d's presence was manifest within the physical realm. However, due to the sin of Adam and Eve concerning the Tree of Knowledge, G-d began to separate Himself from mankind. From this moment onward, the belief in monotheism was weakened and people started worshipping other deities besides the One Creator G-d. Maimonides explains the source of idol worship in his <u>Laws Concerning Idol Worship</u> (ch.1:1). He explains that after Adam, in the generations of Cain, then Enosh etc., mankind mistakenly worshipped the stars and spheres, thinking that they had influence upon the universe.

Indeed, even the Sages state that *"there is not a blade of grass on this material plane that does not have a spiritual force compelling it to grow*[67]*"*. This refers to the fact that every entity within creation has its Divine force that guides it spiritually. Still, these forces are simply like *"an ax in the hand of a chopper*[68]*"*. In other words, although they are great and have a role within the cycle of creation, yet they have no will of their own, except for the one of G-d.

The belief in G-d's uniqueness and oneness continued to decline for seven generations until Abraham initiated the return of G-d's revelation within the physical world. Abraham taught monotheism to his children. This was then bequeathed by Isaac to his son Jacob and so on. Finally, it was Moses, the seventh successor of Abraham, who succeeded in reestablishing an open revelation of G-d's monotheism through the gift of the Torah.

In the following section, we will discuss meditation, but in the context of the Torah. For the experienced meditator, many of the exercises and thoughts expressed may be familiar. This is true, since meditation is a means of attaining spirituality common to many religions and philosophies, as previously discussed. For the inexperienced meditator, this section will prove to be very enlightening in learning how to initiate a meditation. In either case, I hope this section will inspire you with Torah meditations and prove that the gifts of Abraham can truly benefit all of humanity.

It is advisable to meditate at least twice daily. I meditate in the early hours of the morning prior to my morning prayers and again in the evening after finishing work when things are calm at home.

In the evening, I meditate upon my actions of the day. I analyze both the positive and negative situations that I had to deal with. The Sages refer to this as "Cheshbon HaNefesh", the reckoning of the soul. By reinforcing the positive experiences of the day, we reinforce good habits. By recollecting the negative, we isolate our misdeeds and resolve to be better the next day. With the complications of the day settled, we can also look forward to a better night's sleep.

Often, I meditate in the evening following a physical workout. For example, I may run for about 35 minutes, and then meditate for another 35 minutes as I do my stretching exercises. This calms me down and re-orients me after a day full of distractions. Only then can I again focus on what is most important: my connection to my soul.

When my days are extremely busy and filled with pressure, a short period of meditation at midday helps me to maintain a positive attitude. In the practice of law, I am often confronted with a lot of pressure from clients, judges and opposing lawyers. This can become disturbing, especially during a trial. In such circumstances, my associate in law and I may take a short break for a mini-meditation and discussion of a deep Chassidic concept about G-d, creation, or the soul. This helps us avoid being consumed by the problems and obstacles we have to deal with.

Whatever the circumstances, we must make a point of meditating at the times most convenient for us. The best way to do this is by experimenting with different periods of the day, as we experimented with the meditative environment in the previous exercise.

Ideally, meditation should be practiced at fixed hours of the day, just as Jewish prayer takes place at three fixed times during the day. This establishes a routine, allowing meditation to become as important a part of our lives as eating, sleeping and brushing teeth.

Yet, just as our Sages warn us not to let our prayers become too routine, it is also unwise to allow meditation to become too routine. We can avoid this is by not counting the minutes of our meditations, and allowing our sessions to extend freely. The longer our meditations become, the more we will improve our level of concentration.

Even if you choose to meditate for a half hour every single day, it is still beneficial to meditate freely for an extended period of time at least one day a week or month. To enjoy the full flavor of the Jewish meditative experience, meditate for longer periods of time on the holy Sabbath. Besides being designated as a day of rest, The Kabbalah Sages explain that G-d fills the twenty-four hours of the Sabbath with a superior Divine energy non-existent during the other days of the week. The Sabbath is so special that it is said to bless the days of the coming week.

At a minimum, reserve one day a month for long hours of meditation. In Jewish mysticism, the "Sabbath Mevarchim", the Sabbath before the beginning every month that blesses the upcoming month is an ideal time. Similar to the effect of the weekly Sabbath day on the upcoming week, "Sabbath Mevarchim" brings life, vitality and strength to the days of the following month.

My most fruitful meditations occur on the Sabbath, just before the Morning Prayer services, as I meditate on a Chassidic teaching, and again afterwards, when I prolong the Sabbath prayers after other members have gone home. During the morning prior to services, a peaceful atmosphere fills the air, allowing us to express our thoughts freely. At this time, we can meditate to awaken our sense of awareness and thereby improve our level of concentration during the prayers that follow.

Meditation can thus transform our simple prayer for our basic needs into a moment of spiritual bliss.

Meditating on the Sabbath after the prayer service ends can be a very rejuvenating experience, as we can still feel the tremendous energy from the heartfelt prayers throughout the morning filling the synagogue. In our minds, we should try to visualize the energy in the room as wings carrying our own prayers up to heaven.

Although there are auspicious times to meditate, any time is a good time, provided that we are physically and mentally prepared. Practice the previous exercise at different times of the day to discover at which time periods your biorhythms most enhance your meditation.

Physical Postures

The physical position we assume while meditating is critical, as the body that shelters the soul must be very relaxed in order for the soul to fully express itself. The most well known position is the "Lotus", where one sits with legs crossed and the feet above the thighs. If you are not very flexible, it is unadvisable to try to meditate in the Lotus position, as you may find it uncomfortable.

Being able to meditate in a variety of positions is also important. If we become dependent on a single position, we will not enjoy the same levels of concentration and mind control when we are unable to assume that exact position for whatever reason.

During the Jewish morning prayers, there are certain sections of the prayer that must be read while sitting down and others that must be read standing up with our feet together. During the "Amida", which is recited three times daily, we are supposed to stand throughout. Additionally, there are certain verses of the Amida where we bow down to the Al-mighty King of the Universe. It is very common to see a religious worshipper swaying back and forth while deep in prayer.

Swaying helps focus one's mind and let go of any distractions. Others stand in a state of complete stillness in order to focus and unite their energies together. Whichever the preference, it is important to express physically the submission we feel spiritually. The position we assume while meditating symbolizes the goals of that meditation.

Zen Buddhists meditate while walking slowly, since this helps focus the mind and draw energy. We know that Abraham as well as his son Isaac and grandson Jacob spent much time walking their flock of sheep in the mountains where they lived. ZaZen, Tai Chi and other martial arts also practice motion meditation. Yoga has a sweeping array of meditative postures. Students of Yoga often portray the postures of animals, birds or plant life. Examples include the pose of the tree, the warrior, the eagle, the cobra and the fish. As mentioned earlier, these exercises may be practiced according to Jewish religion to gain strength, energy, flexibility and focus, provided that they are disassociated from any form of religious worship.

Before going further, let's experiment with a basic Jewish meditative exercise that will further help you to isolate the most comfortable posture, place and time to meditate:

> *Put on loose, comfortable clothes, which will not make you feel too warm or too cold.*
> *Sit comfortably on a couch or on a pillow on the floor.*
> *Close your eyes and focus your thoughts inward.*
> *Think about how you have been infused with an infinite powerful soul connected to G-d.*
> *Isolate and focus on your great inner strength.*
> *Realize that no matter how complicated certain situations may be in your life, you have been provided with the strength to confront them.*
> *Meditate for as long as you can.*

To get acquainted with your environment, biorhythms and favorite postures, repeat the same exercise at different times during the day and in different postures, sitting down, walking or standing still. Keep notes of which positions and sessions are the most suitable for you, then make them part of your daily routine.

Initiation and Frame of Mind

People erroneously think that by reading about meditation or memorizing a few teachings, one can master the practice. In fact, the Torah states that it took Abraham 99 years to perfect his lofty level of meditation.

There is a saying, *"The principal is the act"*. If we do not personally experience what we read or learn, then we have learned nothing. The knowledge we acquired remains abstract and will never be proven effective.

A successful meditation begins with our realization that within us lies an infinite soul, capable of overcoming any challenge that comes our way. As discussed earlier, G-d's first directive to Abraham was *"Lech Lecha"*- go to yourself. Like Abraham, we all must go toward our essence and the awareness of our true selves.

Yet there is more to the directive *"Go to yourself"* than empowerment through simple self-discovery. The phrase *"Go to yourself"* also implies that to move beyond our physical limitations we must find within ourselves the strength and desire to become better human beings. Since G-d dwells within our infinite souls, by reaching within, we strive to touch the essence of G-d that transcends all barriers and makes such grace possible.

We can start discovering ourselves through meditation by designating a stimulus to focus our attention upon. This will help us to relax and concentrate.

Reciting words of prayer or a passage of the bible, or contemplating on a profound teaching may do the job. Singing or humming a melody or chant (known as a nigun in Hebrew) can also be helpful. Concentrate on the source, meaning, energy and sound of the chant as it occupies your being and emanates through you and your environment. Try the exercise found in the previous section, The Surroundings, this time with intense awareness of the melody or prayer you use to launch your meditation.

Some prefer initiating a meditation by reflecting upon a meaningful picture, listening to contemplative music or smelling pleasant fragrances. In Judaism, one is to be cautious when focusing on an object, since this may be similar to idolatry, an act prohibited according to Torah. In Jewish practice, religious attention should be focused only inward to the one G-d who cannot be seen or heard.

Meditative stimulants should not be regarded as primary objects of focus for ongoing meditation. They should only be used to initiate a certain mood. We should then dispense of them as our meditation deepens. Becoming too dependent on any focus object can lead to us not being able to meditate without it.

The variety of beauty evidenced in G-d's Creation, comprehensible through the senses and the intellect, is so immense and multi-faceted that focusing on one aspect of it alone would limit the quality of our growth. Our selves and our souls are as multi-faceted and bountiful as G-d's infinite wonder surrounding us. Since the stimulants we use have tremendous spiritual meaning for us and become engraved in our souls, the larger the variety we access, the more practice we have in appreciating our own inner multi-faceted, Divine quality.

As an artist, I find drawing extremely relaxing and therefore use it as a technique to initiate meditation. Sometimes, I meditate while taking a walk on the Sabbath.

During these walks, I turn my mind inward and enjoy thinking deeply about the soul, G-d and creation.

The common denominator among meditative stimulants is that they enable us to become absorbed by the given activity or focus. I often admire my children while they play with their toys with full concentration. Their ability to focus on a particular game for a long period of time during imaginative play has always amazed me. Their play is definitely a form of meditation, whereby they sort out the new elements of life they encounter.

In truth, if we are not comfortable in terms of our environment, position and time of day, it will be extremely difficult to meditate, as meditation relies upon our ability to concentrate. Exceptionally, if no stimulants are available, we can initiate a meditation by concentrating on simple, familiar tasks. By not becoming too dependent on the stimulant itself, we allow ourselves the possibility of meditating anywhere and at any time that is convenient to us.

Over the years, I have learned that before trying sophisticated techniques of meditation, it is worthwhile to initiate a meditation with an activity that will easily instigate focus. Once we have reached the right frame of mind by loosening any mental stiffness, proceeding to the next stage becomes natural.

Avoiding Distractions

Abraham gained solitude by hiding in a cave for the most part of his youth. We must not get discouraged if it takes us some time to perfect our level of concentration. If sounds or other disturbances interfere with your meditation, take note of the disturbances and then let them fade out of importance. You may visualize the disturbance as a bird being held in your hand. Imagine that by letting go of the bird, the disturbance escapes into the air and the mind is cleared.

Another way to avoid distracting thoughts during meditation is to focus on the space between each our emotions or daydreams. Focusing on the empty spaces allows us to see the truth about random thoughts – that they are useless and irrelevant. We find this method in the wordless nature of Zen meditation. According to Zen Buddhism, it is in the empty spaces between thoughts where truth is found.

Most of us have lived our lives thinking about everything at once, without any mental direction. It is unfortunate that while our educators have spent so much time feeding us information, they never really took the time to teach us how to use our minds. After all, if our minds functioned properly, we would be better prepared to learn and would be more productive. We would think more positively and be happier.

A few years ago, I learned about a new method of curing people with fatal diseases called "Healing with Laughter". I was told that some doctors treating patients with serious illnesses would take the time to use humor to become close to their patients, thereby strengthening their outlook on life. As a result, many patients greatly improved as they developed more positive attitudes.

Meditation does to a person what no other treatment or exercise can do. After a person has finished a meditation, a sense of clarity and renewed energy is evident. In fact, the more you meditate, the more aware and alert you will be during the course of any other activity. In this way, meditation becomes integrated into our daily lives and is not just one of the many things we must do during a busy schedule of work, family and social life. With practice, meditation naturally enhances our way of thinking and seeing the world.

As an attorney, I appreciate the great value of designing a thorough "preamble" to any contract I draft. Within these paragraphs I set out the overall general rules of conduct and guidelines that the parties should follow before entering into an agreement.

Following a preamble, the contract's rules and obligations are set. However, I find the preamble so important that the first rule I draft in my contract is usually "the preamble is an integral part of the contract". In this way, I assure myself that the parties will realize that it is not enough to only respect the conditions of the contract, but that they should also have the proper attitude while performing their respective obligations. Similarly, meditation is a preamble to life, nourishing and guiding us in much the same way that the preamble does for a contract.

Meditation also helps us observe our own way of thinking and gaining objectivity. When I am having difficulty accomplishing a specific task, I try to step away from myself and become an observer of my own character. By detaching myself, I can see any deficiencies and better rectify them. For example, sometimes while I draw, I become so engrossed in the art I have created that I can no longer see discriminately. At these moments, I usually face my drawing towards a mirror to see the mistakes I have made.

We can learn an important lesson about meditation from the giving of the Torah to the Israelites in the Sinai Desert. G-d would not have given the Torah in just any place, as it was arguably the most important event in the history of the Jewish People. It was then that the Jewish People were united with G-d. G-d chose the desert because it was the most ideal location for the giving of the Torah.

Our Sages offer several explanations why G-d chose the desert as a venue for the giving of the Torah.

Firstly, the desert is ownerless. Similarly, no one person, tribe or category of people can claim exclusive ownership of the Torah. Every individual has equal access to the Torah. Likewise, meditating and contemplating G-d is not exclusively for those of special title, class, creed, gender or credentials. Anyone can grow close to G-d.

Secondly, in the wide open freedom and harsh solitude of the desert, all are equal in their weakness and insignificance. Similarly, to acquire G-d's wisdom through Torah, we must be as humble as we would be in the midst of a desert, relinquishing our egos and all visions of grandeur. To connect with G-d's Eternal Light and discover our true Divine selves through meditation, we must adopt a stance of selflessness in order to free ourselves from the many limiting personal disturbances and labels that consume our daily lives.

Thirdly, just as the Israelites totally depended upon G-d for their sustenance in the desert, we can depend on G-d for personal blessings when we devote ourselves to Torah. In the desert, the ancient Israelites had no resources other than Torah to rely upon. Food, water, clothing and shelter were allocated to them miraculously. Hence, G-d forged a relationship with the ancient Israelites by virtue of their absolute dependence on Him for survival.

Finally, G-d chose to give us the Torah in the barrenness of the desert while we were completely dependent upon Him so that we might viscerally understand both the important power of the Torah and the necessity of humbling ourselves to the One who gave it to us. If during our meditations we are as receptive and open to G-d as the Israelites were in the desert, He will fashion our environment so that it conforms to our good intentions. Similarly, when we approach our meditation with humility, we open ourselves to receiving and embracing the divinity within and around us.

The desert setting is also a metaphor for the sentiment of spiritual emptiness and desolation that we may feel at times. Even when such feelings are justified, we should still not lose hope. Just as G-d gave the Torah in a desert, allowing us to establish a connection to Divinity in the middle of nowhere, we are always given occasion to bond with G-d through Torah and meditation, no matter how empty and naked we may feel spiritually.

Thus, the Torah's meditations can fill all voids. The world, to the naked eye, is like a desert empty of G-d. We must find and reveal G-d everywhere and in everything we do, and by doing so G-d will fill our lives with meaning as he did long ago in the Sinai. By the same token, we must display love and caring to others who feel empty by bringing them closer to Torah.

To become more aware of your thoughts, rid yourself of distractions and open yourself to divinity, try the following exercise:

> *Sit comfortably in a quiet place where you will not be disturbed.*
> *Put on loose clothes so that your body movements are not limited.*
> *Close your eyes and concentrate on relaxing every part of your body, beginning with your facial muscles and ending with your toes.*
> *Focus on how this affects your biorhythms.*
> *Once the body is fully softened, begin to focus on your mind, and become aware of your thoughts and emotions.*
> *At first, let your thoughts and emotions run freely. Then, slowly begin to isolate the empty spaces between every thought.*
> *To build your objectivity, imagine that you are watching a favorite television show, but are focusing only on the commercials advertised and not the actual program. Pretend that your thoughts are the television show itself, and focus instead on the commercials (the emptiness lying between each thought and vision).*

Observe how the thoughts and emotions affect your frame of mind. Do you feel happy, excluded, depressed or nervous? Remember, whatever exists in the mind is only theory until it finds a concrete application. By keeping a negative thought abstract and existing only in the mind, it can be eliminated much more quickly than if it had developed into an action.

The soul, G-d's gift to us, sheds light unto the world. It connects all the pieces together, binding that which is material to the ethereal. Similar to the movement of a candle's flame, your soul reaches toward the heavens while your body keeps you grounded on the earth. Rather than enjoying your light in solitude, share it with the world. The Divine flame within you will only burn stronger.

Chapter 17
Soul Breathing

The Torah compares breath with the Divine Soul. In reference to the creation of man it is written[70]: *"And G-d blew into his nostrils a soul breath of life"*. Indeed, by concentrating on our breathing we can be more in touch with our souls. Conversely, the more aware we are of our soul and its makeup, the better our breathing will be. Breathing is the common denominator connecting the body, mind and soul.

The Kabbalah explains that G-d breathed into Adam a breath of life emanating from His innermost essence. This is confirmed by the statement of the Zohar: *"He who blows, blows from within him"*.

G-d's breathing into man created within him the Divine Soul – Neshama Elokit - a direct extension of G-d.

The Kabbalah discusses the five levels that make up the G-dly soul: "Nefesh" - (soul), "Ruach" - (spirit), "Neshama" - (breath), "Chaya" - (vitality) and "Yechida" - (unity). Starting from the lowest level Nefesh, each soul level is higher and more spiritual until we reach the level of Yechida, the part of the soul that remains fully united with G-d in the higher realms.

"Nefesh" - the aspect of the soul most connected to the physical body, is identified with the bloodstream through which life and vitality flow through the body. We discern this from the Torah verse *"The blood is the Nefesh[71]"*. The word "Nefesh" is also related to the word "Nafshi", meaning "to spread", and relates to the flow of blood spreading throughout the body. The level of Nefesh is reflected in the soul's faculties of thought, speech and action.

"Ruach" - usually interpreted as "the spirit", refers to the emotional characteristics - (middot) - of the soul that mold a person's character. Thus, a happy person is said to have a good spirit and an individual in a bad mood is described as low spirited.

"Neshama" - is the level of the soul most related to the soul's intellectual powers, chochma - (wisdom), bina - (understanding) and da'at - (knowledge). The Hebrew letters that comprise the word "Neshama" also make up the word "Neshima", which means a breath. Just as G-d breathed into Adam a living soul, so too, every person's soul is a result of G-d's Divine breath.

"Chaya" - means life. This refers to the endowment of life and energy for the person from the Al-mighty.

Finally, **"Yechida"** - meaning oneness and unity, depicts the level of the soul which remains united with G-d, untouched and unblemished by the actions or misdeeds of man. The other levels of the soul can also remain united with G-d if they remain unaffected by external influences.

We mentioned that Ruach is the level of the soul which refers to a person's "spirit" and character. However, the word Ruach also has other connotations that connect the themes of breathing, the soul and meditation. Beyond its association with the "spirit" and "personality", Ruach alludes to spirituality in general. For example, a person can be possessed with a Divine Ruach such as in the case of a Tzaddik (Righteous) or a prophet. Such great individuals who have learned to master their thoughts and connect with G-d have "Ruach Hakodesh", the Divine Spirit - an ability that allows them to speak with sublime clarity and precision even regarding future events.

The Prophet Isaiah says that the long awaited Messiah will possess six qualities of Ruach as follows: *"a spirit of wisdom and understanding, a spirit of advice and strength, a spirit of knowledge and awe of G-d[72]"*. In our generation – (the last generation of exile and the first of the Messiah) - it is our duty and privilege to live, breathe and be awakened by this spirit of the Messiah.

At the physical level, "Ruach" also refers to the air we breathe and the wind that blows. Indeed, the element of air is one of the four elements G-d used in the creation of the world[73].

At the beginning of Creation, when the earth was still void and dark, it is written: *"... the breath of G-d hovered over the face of the waters[74]"*. Interestingly enough, immediately afterwards it says: *"And G-d said, 'Let there be light.'"* This points to a causal connection between "air" and "breath" as spirituality and "light", or enlightenment at the human level.

The fact that G-d's breath covered the waters can teach us two things about meditation. Firstly, as the breath of G-d covers the earth, the entire universe is filled with a Divine energy that it is our task to reveal. Secondly, just as water can be cloudy when mixed with dirt or crystal clear when its impurities have settled, so too the mind can be muddled with distracting thoughts or crystal clear when its thoughts are controlled. When the mind is clear, one can achieve a deeper understanding of the self and of life. This is exemplified by G-d creating "light" on the first day of creation prior to the other acts of creation.

In most meditative cultures, breathing is the cornerstone of remaining focused and gaining spiritual insight. In some Eastern practices, it is known as "Pranayama" - the action of releasing and channeling the inner energy found within the body. In Chinese Taoism or Zen, it is known as controlling the "CHI".

The Hindu word "Pranayama" means "the control of prana" - "prana" meaning energy[75]. Pranayama entails evenly distributing a person's level of energy throughout the body and mind. This is very similar to the G-dly attribute of "Tiferet" in Judaism. The root of the Hebrew term "Tiferet" is the word "Pe'er[76]". When spelled in Hebrew, "Pe'er" is comprised of the first three letters of "prana". Like "prana", Pe'er is the balancing of G-d's two most essential qualities: "chesed" - (kindness) and "gevurah" - (strictness), used in the constant energizing of the world and of all existence.

It is said that in the human body, twelve essential channels, each directed to a specific organ, filter CHI. In Tao

From the loins of the intellect spring all that is possible. Wisdom and understanding give birth to feelings of love, awe and admiration of G-d. While the intellect strives to understand G-d, the emotions fuel its mission with intense love and affection. Fill your mind and heart with passion!

Chapter 18
Mastering Intellect and Emotions

With meditation, we can be in harmony with and gain mastery of our intellect and emotions. The tranquility that comes through meditation allows us to focus our minds and utilize our emotions wisely. A peaceful mind will help us avoid being judgmental or negative and will allow us to openly express positive emotions. The Sages tell us that Abraham exemplified the emotion of kindness and conveyed it in many shapes and forms to anyone he met. For example, his home was open to literally thousands of desert travelers who needed a place to eat or sleep.

According to the teachings of Rabbi Schneur Zalman[77], the soul's intellect is divided into three faculties: chochma - (wisdom), bina - (understanding) and da'at - (knowledge). Together they form the Hebrew acronym "ChaBaD."

After an idea has passed through these three intellectual faculties, it will then arouse any of the soul's middot - (emotions). These emotional faculties include feelings such as love, fear, compassion, severity, pride, victory, etc. After the intellect arouses an emotion, the original thought is then acted upon through the three "garments" of the soul: thought, speech and action.

In psychological terms, the above-mentioned expressions of the soul would be referred to as the "conscious" and symbolize the interrelationship between the ChaBaD and the emotions. On the other hand, the "unconscious" encompasses memory, imagination, previous experiences and stored or forgotten knowledge. Within the unconscious lie the causes of many of the things we do, think or say that we may not necessarily have explanations for. Between the "conscious" and the "unconscious", there is also a "go between" level which psychologists refer to as the "preconscious". The preconscious facilitates the transfer of knowledge from the hidden to the revealed.

In a similar vein, our G-dly souls possess memories of past experiences and forgotten knowledge. According to Judaism, before our soul descended from the spiritual realm to enter our bodies, it enjoyed a tremendous closeness to and love for G-d. Also, it is traditionally believed that our G-dly soul knew the entire Torah prior to its decent to this world, when an angel caused it to forget its Torah knowledge.

The "preconscious" that transfers hidden knowledge from our G-dly soul to our conscious mind also stirs us to love and fear G-d and to follow in His ways. During the transition, the positive experiences of the past stimulate our "Ratzon" - (will) - to constantly improve our behavior.

This supports the accepted notion that we possess the information and intellectual tools necessary to handle most of life's problems. However, in order to activate these hidden treasures, it is often important to stimulate our minds through meditation.

Through meditation, we become more aware of the reasons why we feel fear, pain, sadness or other emotions. When we find ourselves in a state of depression, we can explore the reservoir of our unconscious and uncover the memory of a past spiritual or physical incident to empower ourselves. In a sense, our unconscious is much like a filing cabinet full of important information necessary to guide our lives. The practice of meditation hones our ability to quickly locate and apply the most appropriate information from within the filing cabinet.

The mind has the ability to influence our emotions, and it should do so rather than allowing feelings to take over our lives. This does not imply that we should never be sensitive or react with feelings of love or awe. Rather, it means that in order for us to avoid becoming emotionally reacting individuals, the mind should direct the arousal and calming of our feelings when appropriate.

The mind in its entirety is filled with a plethora of conflicting thoughts, emotions and ideas, some revealed and some hidden. Many of the thoughts, emotions and ideas that pass through our minds like clouds in the sky do not necessarily represent what we really feel, think or want. Most often, they are transient emotional responses to circumstances we are experiencing. The worst thing we can do is to act upon these temporary ideas. Although we feel a certain way about a particular thought today, we probably felt completely differently yesterday and may feel differently again tomorrow. By making us aware of our thoughts, meditation allows us to prioritize and control them, transforming our negative reactions into positive actions.

When thinking of a troubling matter or an aggravating person, we may feel anxiety, anger or hostility. On the other hand, bringing to mind a happy memory or future plan elicits feelings of happiness and enthusiasm. Thoughts of family and close ones arouse feelings of love, compassion and attachment.

Thus, by learning to control our emotions through meditation, we can greatly reduce the influence disappointing situations or persons will have on our lives.

The Baal Shem Tov teaches us yet another very interesting lesson about humanity. When we see a fault in someone else, it is only because the fault exists within ourselves. Therefore, before criticizing or trying to correct the fault in someone else, we must first rectify it within our own being.

Since every unpleasant emotion arises from a negative thought, we must eliminate these unwanted thoughts prior to transforming the negative emotions associated with them. According to Judaism, negative situations are not intended to harm us, since they come from G-d. They are merely stumbling blocks sent from heaven to induce us to reveal our hidden resources and become more focused. G-d does not give us insurmountable challenges. If we are faced with a situation, then we must have the resources to deal with it.

Asking ourselves questions can greatly relax us by facilitating our understanding of a situation. The more peaceful and relaxed we become, the easier it is for us to effectively resolve the matter at hand. We must ask: Why am I feeling this way? Am I overreacting in this situation? Does the situation really change my circumstances and in what way? Is the problem as bad as I feel it to be? Do I represent the emotion being felt of fear, anxiety, depression, or resentment? Do I need to dwell in my emotions when dealing with the circumstance, or will it be better resolved if I eliminate these stubborn feelings? Can I perhaps grow from the situation being experienced? Ignoring the depths of our thoughts can lead to living a shallow life.

Each of us has been infused with a Divine Soul. Although we can't always see the positive soul potential in some people, with meditation we can still establish a bond of love with every human being. Knowing that our souls all come from the same Divine source and that we all share the same union with G-d, we realize that whatever is good for the self is also good for others. On the other hand, if we harm another person, it is as though we harm ourselves. In keeping with Jewish thought, there is no real separation between people. On the contrary, the differences that exist between people are viewed as the source of a limitless variety of positive contributions to the human race.

Although in general, the mind should influence the emotions, positive feelings must always be permitted to rule over the intellect. For example, when we see someone in need, we must arouse within ourselves feelings of compassion, love and kindness. By meditating on our true nature, we enable our most positive feelings to rule our thoughts and actions for the benefit of all.

In the Talmud[78] our Sages state that *"A person who gives a coin to a poor person is granted six blessings; (however,) he who honors (a poor person) is given eleven blessings."* "Honoring" does not necessarily mean to give more money. Rather, it implies giving a positive feeling to the other by sharing warmth and love. Thus, giving of our time, mind and feelings to another is a greater act of kindness than giving of our funds. I know a rabbi who says: *"It's a lot easier to write a check for a good cause than to volunteer your time."*

The Baal Shem Tov said that a soul may come down to this world for seventy or eighty years just to do one favor for another person.

The Torah tells us that the purpose of every being is to shed light and kindness into the world. Particularly, we each have a specific area on earth that we can and should rectify. Because it is difficult to know which of our acts was our raison d'être, ideally we should fill our lives with acts of kindness.

The Lubavitcher Rebbe, Rabbi Menachem Mendel Schneerson explained this concept as follows: Every piece of the world waits impatiently for its redeemer. Without the help of a specific individual, it is impossible for that part of the world to reach its fulfillment. With our cumulative acts of goodness and kindness, we can bring redemption to the whole world. Through meditation, we can positively guide our every thought, word and deed toward the intent of bringing positive change to the world.

Choose neither the soul over the body, nor the body over the soul. When you indulge or deprive either, you betray your Father in Heaven who has intended that soul and body unite in healthy harmony to serve Him. Without the vessel of the body to sustain life and carry us toward G-d, the soul cannot fulfill its mission to serve as our guiding beacon throughout life.

Chapter 19
The State of the Body

People often think that meditation is only beneficial to mind and spirit. The truth is that meditation enables us to isolate and cure what ails us physically in much the same way that it does emotionally, intellectually and spiritually. Through meditation, a person can not only better perceive and control what is within the mind and soul, but also what exists within the vessel that contains them – the body. The Torah tells us that after Abraham had circumcised himself at the age of 99 years old, he sat at the entrance of his house anxiously waiting to fulfill a good deed towards another. The fact that he was in immense pain did not discourage him from wanting to receive people at his house. Through his deep focus in this vein, he merited a visit by G-d on the third day following his circumcision (Genesis 18:1).

From the time we are born until the day we pass on, we are constantly assuming habits, many of which are good for us and many more that are not so good. We do not usually pay much attention to these habits or what our minds and bodies consume. Sometimes we do not posture properly, speak clearly or control our emotional responses to daily situations. As a result, we simply do not know how to redirect our habits. Thus over time, some of us avoid exercising and get out of shape, while others develop drug and alcohol addictions and eating disorders. Simply put, because we are not paying attention, most of us are not living the best and healthiest lives possible.

Consistent meditation sessions result in many physical benefits. Among other things, meditation yields added energy to the body, increased control over our organs, a cure to insomnia, lowered blood pressure, reduced fatigue, and better physical balance. Best yet, meditation makes us more aware of our habits and, through this new awareness, puts us well on the road to curbing them.

Meditation also relaxes the nervous system and leads the body to function more competently. By focusing on answers within the self, meditation empowers the body to avoid outside addictions while improving its ability to cure itself and completing any of its deficiencies.

Meditation allows a person to become more aware of his bodily organs and movements. In fact, every movement a person makes can be the focus or subject of a meditation. The Sages tell us that through meditation, Abraham gained mastery over his sensory organs, which normally are uncontrollable.

My wife, who regularly does yoga-like exercises, tells me that when she concentrates on her exercises, she is able to tune into the various motions she makes and can direct her bodily energies more efficiently. She has also disciplined our family to exercise regularly and to eat well-balanced meals. In fact, if one of our children is feeling under the weather, before going to a doctor, she will first try some natural remedies. She often uses breathing techniques or healing through transmission of energy, referred to in some circles as "reiki". Transmission of energy is achieved by placing a hand on the part of the body that is hurting and concentrating on disseminating energy into that area. This type of meditation actually works!

The reiki or transmission of energy that my wife uses to heal our children is not limited to gurus. Even my five-year-old daughter Mayan has learned some of these techniques and uses them on her siblings when they are not well.

It is comforting to note that within the marvelous bodies G-d created for us, He included many of the remedies for the illnesses we may contract. The body has an immune system naturally capable of healing itself. With the help of medicine and doctors, this system is accelerated and fine-tuned. However, if the body does not cooperate or react to a medication, then even a doctor will not be able to heal the problem.

When we meditate on the body, we should visualize it as a home for the G-dly soul. That is, just as a physical dwelling, a body should feel comfortable, spacious and organized.

In Judaism, punishing the body is never a recommended method of discipline. Extended fasting, sleep deprivation, defying inclement weather and the like are prohibited. Since the body is the vehicle for the soul, a weak body will negatively affect the soul. On the other hand, when the body is energized, it can better fulfill the mission of the soul encased within it.

To best care for the G-dly soul, we must intentionally eat properly and exercise regularly. When the body has been well maintained, we are better able to serve our Master above.

Likewise, the way we start our morning will make a big difference in the way our day turns out. It is therefore essential to begin the day by orienting the body and soul in proper perspective.

The Code of the Jewish Law offers very useful meditations to practice when rising in the morning[79]:

> *In the morning, a person should begin his day by thanking the Al-mighty for returning his soul after a night of sleep. During the day one should think about the following verse: "I place G-d before me at all times (Psalm 16:8)." This is a major principle of the Torah and a path of the righteous who proceed before G-d.*
>
> *The way a person lives, acts, and deals when he is alone in his home differs from his behavior when he is in the presence of a great king. Similarly, his manner of talking with his household and close circle differ from his speech and manner of talking when he is in the king's chambers. Then, he takes care that all his acts and words are correct and proper.*

The same applies when a person becomes aware that the great King, the Holy One, Blessed be He, whose "glory fills the entire world[80]" stands over him and observes his deeds. This is as it states: "Can a person hide in the secret places without my seeing him,' says the L-rd; 'behold, I fill up the heavens and earth[81].'" This realization should immediately prompt awe and humility resulting from fear of G-d, blessed is He, and cause one to feel shame because of Him.

Similarly, when lying on his bed, a person should realize before whom he is laying. Immediately, upon rising from sleep, he should recall the kindness that G-d, blessed is He, performs for him, returning his soul. He entrusts his soul to G-d tired, and G-d returns it to him renewed and rested, so that he can carry out his service with all of his potential and serve Him the entire day. "This is the totality of man's purpose for existence[82]."

It is stated[83]: "Renewed in the morning, great is your faithfulness." This implies that every morning, a person is renewed as a new creation. Therefore, he should thank G-d, Blessed be He, for this with all his heart. While he is still on his bed, he should recite Modeh Ani: "I offer thanks to You, living and eternal king, for having mercifully restored my soul within me. Great is your faithfulness." This may be recited even though one's hands are not clean for it does not contain any of the names of G-d.

Yehudah ben Tema would say: "Be bold like a leopard and swift like an eagle, run like a deer, and brave like a lion to do the will of your Father in heaven[84]." "Bold like a leopard" implies that a person should not be embarrassed before the people who scoff at his service of G-d, Blessed be He.

"Swift like an eagle" relates to a person's sight, teaching that he should be swift to close his eyes when he sees evil - for that is the beginning of sin. The heart desires, the eyes see, and the limbs complete the act.

"Run like a deer" relates to one's feet. One's feet should run to do good.

"Brave like a lion" relates to the heart. The courage required in the service of G-d is rooted in the heart. This teaches that a person should apply his heart to do His service, overcome the evil inclination, and be victorious over it, as a mighty man overcomes his enemy, conquering him, and throwing him to the ground.

Even if he finds this difficult because of the heaviness and laziness of the body, he should place the will of the King of Kings, the Holy One, Blessed be He, as his goal. He should think to himself that if he were called to a business matter, to collect a debt, or to save his money he would surely get up eagerly, without any hesitation because of the love for his money. Similarly, if he had to report to a king's service, he would get up eagerly, without hesitation, out of fear that others would betray him, or because of his desire to find favor in the king's eyes.

How much more so he should take care to rise with speed and eagerness to the service of the King of Kings, the Holy One, Blessed is He. Once a person trains himself to do this four or five times, it will not be so difficult for him because "a person who comes to purify himself is helped[85]."

The above concepts point to the importance of waking up with the awareness that G-d has entrusted us with a Divine

Soul in order to know Him with our physical bodies in all our endeavors.

According to Jewish Law the first thing we must do when rising from sleep is to wash our hands. This is because during our sleep, a portion of our soul ascends above and a spirit of impurity descends upon the body. When we awake from our sleep, the spirit of impurity leaves the body with the exception of the fingers. This impurity does not pass until we purify our hands with water.

When we meditate on the "Modeh Ani" prayer: *"I thank You Living and Eternal King for restoring to me my soul with mercy, great is the belief in You"*, we recognize G-d's kindness in returning our soul to our body.

We must take the time when rising in the morning to appreciate the gift of life. We should not take for granted our power of touch, of sight, of hearing and of smell. We should try to wake up in a relaxed way, feeling the renewed energy that enters our body. This may, at first, be difficult to appreciate. With practice, however, such awareness becomes natural.

During the day while you are at home, work or school, pay attention to what you do and how you do it, to what you say and how you say it, to what you hear and how you understand it.

When dealing with stressful situations, notice how your body reacts by either tightening up or by becoming more rigid. Also see how your posture or tone of voice may change. Realize that you are never confronted with a situation that you cannot handle. Know that if you are exposed to a problem it is only because you have the tools to deal with it.

To increase your awareness of and control over your body, try the following relaxation exercise:

Sit comfortably, and focus on your left hand. Begin by staring at your palm for a few seconds. Now,

move around each of your fingers beginning with your thumb.
Relax your hand and start focusing on your right foot. To initiate concentration, wiggle your toes for a few seconds.
Repeat the same exercise for every body part. Become aware of your chest, your abdomen, your eyes, ears, and nose etc. Familiarize yourself with every organ of your body, paying attention to the different sensations felt.
Ask yourself; how does each body part feel in and of itself. Do I feel any tension in my body? (If you do, concentrate on releasing it as if you were undoing a knot.)
As you meditate on each part of your body, focusing on the function of each, realize that each body part is energized by the Divine Soul enclothed within the body. Visualize this flow of Divine energy as being initiated with your breath and then spreading throughout the body.
As your breath of energy is occupying your head, chest and arms, think of it now going even lower into every body part until it is felt even in the toes.
Once you have meditated on your breath spreading throughout the body, imagine now that as you inhale, your body is being filled with this breath of life.

The above exercise can be very uplifting and reinforcing. With practice, you will be able to tap into the energy that flows throughout your body. Thus, if a part of your body feels weak, it is probably because your energy is not properly penetrating it. Once you isolate the problem area, focusing on reducing the rigidity by channeling the energy of your soul into it. With practice, you can become more aware of every part of your body, able to see and feel how each functions individually and in conjunction with other parts of your body.

The next easy exercise will help you to foster harmony between the various parts of your body.

> *Close your eyes and sit comfortably.*
> *Focus on the motion of your breath for a moment, carefully observing how you exhale and inhale. (Try this for at least 1 minute)*
> *Now as you inhale, visualize your breath filling your head, going through your mind and surrounding all your thoughts.*
> *While focusing on the breath filling your head, visualize it being drawn through the neck (as if it was a funnel) into your chest, hands, body and feet.*
> *Now visualize the soul's energy flowing through each of your organs individually.*

Practice this exercise regularly to become more aware of the use and functioning of each part of your body. You will quickly realize that the harmonious interaction of the parts of your body is as important as the unity and collaboration of people within human society. Be ever mindful that much like the parts of a body, each human being has a vital function to fulfill and we all must work harmoniously with others in order to connect with the Divine force that sustains us all.

Nothing escapes G-d. He is mindful and aware of all things. For fate to truly be a blessing, reciprocate His state of awareness by becoming more conscious of His presence and direct influence.

Chapter 20
Divine Providence

In Judaism, as in many other religions, meditation serves to liberate the mind and soul from all constraints and allow for limitless Divine expression as it enables the practitioner to become more focused and aware. Yet ultimately, when we meditate to connect with G-d, our focus and awareness takes on a more sublime meaning. We evoke Divine energy. The Midrash tells us that one of the greatest tests endured by Abraham was when he was condemned to be burned to death in a fiery furnace. Rather than being consumed by the great fire, Abraham emerged untouched and with unprecedented energy.

Chassidic philosophy explains that this energy, latent in all physical things, has a spiritual counterpart in existence since the creation of the world. Due to this symbiotic relationship - akin to a Trekkian parallel universe, everything that happens in the material world has a purpose and impacts on the spiritual realm. Moreover, nothing we experience in the physical world is unique or original. All that we experience physically is but a concrete manifestation of its spiritual equivalent as popularized in recent bestsellers such as "The Celestine Prophecy".

At this point, I'd like to share with you the following story as it will help ground this lofty philosophy in a reality we all can relate to. Sometime in the late 1800s, a revered Rebbe (Chassidic Master) invited a well-known psychology professor to his home to partake in his Sabbath feast. During the meal the professor excitedly began explaining new discoveries related to the development of memory and concentration to his host. The Rebbe patiently listened to his guest until he was finished. Without saying a word, the Rebbe then went into his study and soon emerged with an old manuscript written by one of his predecessors. He opened the dusty Chassidic manuscript and quickly referred to the exact same ideas the professor had just so enthusiastically shared. To the professor's amazement, the

Rebbe pointed out the sections that discussed a vein in the brain affecting one's memory and focus. When the professor asked if the Rebbe had been a scientist, the Rebbe responded in the negative, stating that he understood the brain because it already existed in the spiritual realm, long before scientific discovery.

Jewish Sages explain that prior to the creation of the world, G-d contemplated upon the purpose of every one of its details. He also placed His Divine thought into the making of the physical world, with the intention of causing this realm to be a dwelling place for the Divine. Meditation is therefore not a human invention but rather a G-dly one. Contemplation, thought and intention are some of the key elements that make up G-d's meditation. In the following sections we will be discussing G-d's meditation, how it affects us and also how our meditation affects G-dliness as we become more aware of His presence or observe His Torah.

In conversation between Jews, one often hears the expression that a certain event happened by "Hashgacha Pratit" – Divine Providence. Divine Providence means that G-d intends everything to happen exactly as it does, and that G-d contemplates every minute detail of His creation. Nothing happens without reason and everything serves a purpose in G-d's infinite creation. Even those things that appear negative or evil on the surface are in truth positive and good. Due to their very lofty nature, certain events must sometimes be cloaked in negativity[86].

The Baal Shem Tov explains the Chassidic view on Divine Providence in the following way:

> *G-d's providence governs every minute creation, even a fallen leaf that has been tossed over and over by the wind or a bit of straw that someone used when thatching a roof some years ago. To move them from one place to another a storm-wind erupts, shaking heaven and earth in the middle of a warm sunny day to bring fulfillment to the Divine Providence that*

governs this small stray leaf and old wisp of straw. The movement of a single blade of grass in the depths of a forest, on a stately mountain or in a deep valley where man has never passed, to its right or to its left, is determined throughout its entire life according to Divine Providence.

G-d, Blessed be He, decreed that a particular blade of grass will live for a specific number of months, days and hours, and that for the duration of this period it will turn and bend a certain number of times...

The movement of this particular blade of grass effects creation in its entirety, allowing G-d's intent in creation to come to fulfillment.

Chassidic philosophy explains that there are two general types of Divine Providence[87]: External Divine Providence – (Hashgacha Chitzonit) - and Inner-directed Divine Providence – (Hashgacha Pnimit).

Inner-directed Divine Providence refers to G-dly influence that is open and revealed – not concealed in nature. This Divine Providence can be felt especially when we purposefully connect with G-d through prayer and meditation.

External Divine Providence refers to the G-dly influence hidden and concealed within the laws of nature, a seemingly more passive G-dly involvement. This Divine Providence governs all other entities – animal, vegetable, inanimate – and those who choose not to connect with G-d at all.

Since G-d is mindful and aware of all things that take place in the world, it is incumbent upon us to reciprocate this state of awareness by becoming more conscious of G-d's presence and direct influence on the world. The deeper we meditate and contemplate these concepts, the closer we connect to G-d, and the more we can tap into the G-dly essence concealed within us.

Traditionally, mindfulness implies that one is acutely aware of all of one's encounters in order to develop a better understanding of life. However, in Judaism, being mindful takes on a more sublime character since it means seeing G-d's involvement in everything that happens. Particularly, "enlightenment" according to Judaism implies a connection with the Divine energy that vitalizes all physical matter. Only when we are enlightened - aware of G-d's constant guidance in leading us to our personal destiny - can we forge a close connection and intimate relationship with Him.

Since according to Jewish thought, G-d affects everything that happens and G-d is "All Good", everything that happens below must also be good. There is a common saying, *"what comes easy, goes easy"*. Jewish Sages say: *"According to the effort, such is the reward"*. Thus, the fulfillment of Divine Providence entails that we focus on bringing out the positive dimension concealed in every situation we encounter. Through our meditations on the deep intrinsic relationship that exists between heaven and earth and between the spiritual and material, we solidify our relationship with G-d as we become increasingly aware of His involvement.

As mentioned earlier, Chassidic philosophy teaches that everything that exists physically does so because it already has its counterpart in spirituality. Thus, when there is a physical change, it has originated in an awakening in the spiritual realm. Through meditation, our awareness of this material-spiritual symbiosis is enhanced and in turn this enhanced awareness enables us to become receptive vessels for Divine intervention in the material world.

Hinduism refers to this hidden power as "Prana" – the hidden force revealed through man's physical activity. This may be similar to the Hebrew word Pe'er that derives from the root word "Tiferet" found in the Kabbalah. Tiferet - (beauty or glory of G-d) - is the level revealing the hidden sublime forces of kindness and judgment which animates the world and allows for its continued existence.

Since everything we do and say has an impact upon what happens both in the physical and in the spiritual realms, it is crucial that we become aware of our tremendous power and develop a positive attitude in keeping with the adage that everything that happens is for the good. When we are aware, mindful and enlightened, we naturally realize that everything that occurs is good and for our benefit. Even though the positive side of a situation is not always obvious, by thinking and acting positively, we can activate the revelation of that event's essential goodness.

In the Talmud, there are two stories that shed light on the Jewish concept of Divine Providence. Tractate Berachot[88] relates the following story: Rabbi Akiva was once traveling with a candle, a donkey and a rooster. The candle was to provide light so that he could study Torah at night, the donkey was for traveling, and the rooster was in order to wake him at dawn for prayers.

One evening, a very weary Rabbi Akiva stopped in a small town looking for a place to spend the night. However, the town's people did not welcome him or offer him a place to rest. Rabbi Akiva had no choice but to sleep in the forest outside the town. During the night, a lion came and devoured his donkey. Now, he had no way to travel. Then a cat ate his rooster. Now, he would not be able to wake himself at dawn. Then a wind blew out his only candle, making it impossible for him to learn Torah that night. To each of these difficulties, Rabbi Akiva responded with the expression, *"Everything G-d does, He does so for the good"*.

When Rabbi Akiva awoke the next morning, he discovered that indeed everything was for the good. During the night, while Rabbi Akiva slept in the forest, bandits invaded the town, robbing and murdering all of the inhabitants. Had he been allowed to sleep in the town, had his candle been lit, had his donkey or rooster been alive and made noise, the bandits would have discovered Rabbi Akiva and killed him as well. Thus, because of the loss of his donkey, rooster and candle, his life was spared.

The second story found in the Talmud involves a Sage known as Nachum "Ish Gam Zu" – Nachum, the man who says *"this too is for the good"*.

On behalf of the Jewish community, Nachum was sent to Rome on an important mission to appease Caesar. Nachum was given a chest of precious stones to bring as a present to the king.

Along the way, he stayed overnight at a certain inn. In the middle of the night, the precious stones were stolen from his chest and replaced with dirt. In the morning, he discovered the switch that had taken place. He said: *"This too is for the good"* and continued on his way to deliver the chest full of dirt to Caesar!

He arrived before the king and the chest was opened. When Caesar saw that he was given a chest full of dirt, he became enraged and exclaimed: *"The Jews are mocking me!"* He ordered Nachum to be killed immediately. Still, Nachum said *"This too is for the good"*.

Just then, Elijah the Prophet appeared to the guards disguised as a Roman minister. He said: *"Perhaps this dirt is from the dirt of our father Abraham; For Abraham would throw dirt and it would turn into swords"*. The Romans tested some of the dirt and found that it was so. At the time, Rome was engaged in many wars and conquests. There was one particular area they were having trouble controlling. The Romans threw some of the dirt at the defenders of the city and easily conquered it. Now, Nachum was treated as a hero. He was taken into the king's treasure vault and told to take as he pleased. Nachum filled his chest with gold and left in great honor.

Sit in a comfortable position in a quiet place.
Close your eyes and slowly take a few deep breaths.
Envision the challenging situation before your eyes for a few moments.
Say to yourself, "Everything G-d does, He does so for the good" or alternatively "This too is for the good" (repeat this pronouncement for a few minutes).
Realize that everything that occurs within the physical world is a consequence from above.
Think to yourself: Since G-d is mindful and aware of all things which take place in the world, it is my obligation to reciprocate this state of awareness by becoming more conscious of His presence and direct influence within my life. (The deeper you meditate on this idea, the easier it will be to connect to G-d and tap into the G-dly essence concealed within your being.)
Visualize G-d's involvement in the present challenge, saying to yourself that since G-d is all good and eternally reasonable, everything He causes must also be good.
Deepen your experience by intensifying your awareness of G-d's involvement and the hidden good within the situation you are facing.
Visualize your challenge once again, this time isolating the potential good implicit within the situation. Realize that sometimes, great blessings will reveal themselves in a negative form only because they are too lofty to grasp without challenge.
Allow your mind and heart to become aware of G-d's presence and realize that He hears, oversees and influences every step you take.
Now look forward to experiencing and overcoming the difficult situation.

Thank G-d for giving you the opportunity to face such challenges, since now you have discovered your true inner potential.

Repeat this exercise several times if necessary. Eventually with the help of G-d, any apparent negative situation you may experience will transform into a positive one.

Some try to belittle pain by explaining that suffering is just part of what people have to go through in life. Others utilize suffering to justify their negative or improper attitudes and actions. In reality, no explanation can completely satisfy our limited understanding of the cause of humanity's suffering. However, G-d's understanding is far beyond our own and we must therefore develop complete trust in G-d and believe that everything He does is good. By realizing that G-d is good in every detail of life, we can move on with less worry and confusion.

Let us consider an analogy: If a man were to awake suddenly and feel the pressure of a cool blade on his chest, he would presumably panic. If, however, in the next moment he realizes that he is on an operating table and the cool blade belongs to a friendly and caring surgeon, he will feel a lot better. Even though he has no idea what the surgeon is doing, he knows it is being done for his good.

Likewise, first and foremost, we should accept that all G-d does is for the good and meditate on the goodness of G-d. We must remind ourselves of all the good things G-d has created in this world and the kind way in which He has sustained all of His creations. Upon contemplation, we can also find the many blessings G-d has bestowed upon our own personal lives. We can only conclude that trying situations also derive from G-d and therefore must be good, albeit in a concealed way.

Always remember that trying situations can serve a purpose in and of themselves when they motivate us to realize their Divine origins and understand that they are a concealed expression of G-d's infinite goodness.

The pain, suffering, evil and negativity we encounter do not exist separate of G-d. G-d created the appearance of evil to provide us with a challenge. When we react in an appropriate way, the difficult situation can transform itself into a positive one.

Since all of our challenges are presented by G-d, it follows that they cannot be insurmountable. Our Sages tell us that G-d has provided us with the ability to overcome. G-d is good and would not present us with an impossible challenge.

After understanding that G-d is good and that there is good to be found in every circumstance, we can use four meditations to explore the positive aspects of pain and suffering. One or more of these meditations may be more appropriate in a given situation, based on the circumstance and the type of individual. If, for whatever reason, these meditations do not yield a proper state of mind, we must still trust that G-d is good and all that He does is for the good.

The following four meditations called "The Challenge", "Arousing Hidden Strengths", "Cleansing the Soul" and "Revealing Greater Good" will empower you to overcome challenge, pain and suffering in the most positive manner possible. The mantras in general have been inspired by King David's book of Psalms. Prior to beginning each exercise, it is important to carefully read the associated section until its essential message becomes clear to you. To begin each exercise, sit in a comfortable position where it is quiet, close your eyes and breathe deeply. Visualize your situation for a few moments and then contemplate on the explanations given for each of the following meditations. Use the mantras at the end of each explanation to initiate and guide your meditation.

The Challenge

G-d could have created a world without any pain and suffering where only good is manifested. This would seemingly make more sense, since the negative feelings resulting from difficulties can be an obstacle to our attachment to Divinity. Instead, G-d created a world that resembles a mixture of good, evil, pain and joy. He did this so that man would be faced with challenges, as without challenge, we would never have cause to tap into our latent powers usually reserved for exceptional circumstances. Manifesting these hidden strengths causes a similar reaction above whereby G-d is tempted to also go beyond minimal providence for us.

When we are challenged by difficult circumstances, it is easy to blame others for our misfortune, reject G-d, or resort to anger, depression and other improper behaviors. Alternatively, we can reach out to G-d, follow in his ways and pray to Him. When we choose the latter, we please G-d by helping to make the world a dwelling place for Him. To afford us this empowering choice, G-d created the world.

G-d had no need for anything, including the creation of the physical world. His desire in creation was motivated by His desire to share His goodness with mankind. For this reason, following the creation of man, the Torah states: *"And G-d saw all that He made and behold it was very good[91]"*. The Sages explain that prior to the creation of the world G-d had consulted with the "Souls" to discuss the best way to make a common home for Him and for us. In light of this thought, the Sages have explained that in the verse *"Let us create man in our image and in our liking"* the word "us" refers to both G-d and the Souls.

Suffice it to say that if G-d had created only good in this world, being and doing good wouldn't have been a challenge, since there would have been no other choice. Only in a world covered with layers of darkness can we choose light and enjoy its rewards.

Mantra To Overcome Challenges:
G-d is all good, caring and merciful. Everything He does is good.
In His wisdom, G-d has given me this challenge for my good.
In His mercy, G-d has given me the strength and courage to overcome this challenge.
I have the will and courage to persevere!

Arousing Hidden Strengths

Now that we've used "The Challenge" meditation to recognize the hidden goodness in every situation and our innate ability to overcome it, the "Arousing Hidden Strengths" meditation will make obvious the important reason for our challenges. By practicing this exercise, we can arouse our hidden strengths and become a better person as a result of our difficulties.

When we realize that our difficulties are meant to present us with a challenge that we too have the ability overcome, we unearth our G-d-given powers and strengths to face the challenge and respond positively. These powers are hidden so deeply within us that until we have been confronted with a trying situation we were unaware of their very existence. By discovering and arousing these treasures, we become better people.

When faced with a challenge, we can either strive to succeed with our G-d given energies or fail. For example, when lacking the barest of necessities, some people will become selfish and resort to stealing. Others find within themselves more sympathy for those who have even less than they do. During times of war, people have murdered their friends for a morsel of bread. Others shared the little that they had. When sick, some may tune out the rest of the world. Others choose to seek out people who are more unfortunate than they are or join the effort to find a cure. The choice is always ours. We can use any experience as an opportunity to become a better person.

There are many well-known examples to consider. The nationwide organization MADD (Mothers Against Drunk Driving) was founded by a mother who suffered the tragic loss of a beloved child to a drunk driver. Similarly, victims of Breast Cancer, Lupus, Parkinson's disease, domestic abuse and other trials have become champions of those causes, devoting *be punished on my account...May the words of my mouth and the meditation of my heart be acceptable before You, L-rd who is my Strength and my Redeemer."*

This prayer is then followed by a series of verses from the bible and psalms which encourage placing our trust in G-d alone. One example of such prayer meditated upon each night is:

"Our Father, let us lie down in peace, our King raise us up to a good life and peace. Improve us with Your good counsel, help us speedily for the sake of Your Name and spread over us the shelter of Your peace. Protect us from the enemy. Remove the adversary from before us and from behind us. Shelter us in the shadow of Your wings and guard our going out and our coming in for a good life and peace from now and for all time. For You benevolent G-d are our guardian and our deliverer."

There are several levels of truth. Every person was created in the image of G-d. Each individual resembles the Almighty. For truth to be eternal, it must be true for all those created in the image of G-d, past, present and future, here and everywhere. This level of truth can only be perceived when all of creation is viewed with the eyes of the soul, instead of with the eyes of the body alone.

Chapter 22
To Know G-d

Generally, the goal of all meditation is to attain a higher awareness of our spirituality and soul. Indeed, meditation and contemplation are vehicles for bringing us closer to knowing G-d. In a mystical work called Raya Mehemna[97], the author explains that Abraham's close relationship with G-d's Divine presence known as the "Shechina" was comparable to that of a father (Abraham) towards his daughter (the Shechina). Concerning Moses however, the Shechina is referred to as his wife. This demonstrates how close we can come to G-d.

The first of G-d's Ten Commandments given on Mount Sinai was: *"I am the Lord your G-d[98]"*. Maimonides writes at the very beginning of his Code of Jewish Law: *"The foundation of all foundations, and pillar of all wisdom, is to know that there is a First Existence who brings all other existence into being[99]."* This statement teaches us important lessons about Torah meditation, notably that the goal of meditation is to become one with G-d and to perceive His presence within the physical realm. Through meditation, we realize not only that G-d is actively involved with every part of our lives, but also that He resides within the recesses of our hearts and souls.

Maimonides defines G-d as a being whose existence is dependent on nothing else and the existence of all other things is contingent upon Him. Every bit of matter in the world down to the last sub-atomic particle is created by G-d and depends on Him for continued existence. This makes G-d the only necessary being and true existence. As Maimonides writes further: *"His truth is not like the truth of any single other thing[100]."*

Chassidic philosophy explains that "metziuso meatzmusa" – G-d's existence comes from His very own essence. When Moses asked G-d to define Himself, He replied,

"I Am Who I Am[101]*."* In other words, G-d is the Being that He chooses to be, but not for any reason we can fathom.

Prior to the creation of the world, G-d existed alone. His presence filled every conceivable space. Then G-d created the world. Yet, nothing was subtracted from G-d's existence and space. The world, being G-d's creation, remains united with G-d and dependent on Him for its existence. This constant unity between the unlimited and spiritual and the limited and physical defies understanding. While G-d is unique and above all, He is still one with His creations. The process of creation is not something that took place only at the beginning of the world; it is something that re-occurs continuously. If G-d were to cease creating the world for one second it would return to the void it was prior to its creation[102]. Through being aware of G-d and fulfilling acts of goodness, man is a partner in this unity, arousing within Him a will to continue energizing the world.

Meditation and contemplation are the important tools we need to become mindful and aware of G-d's constant presence.

The reality we know of before meditating on G-d is the world of physical and mundane entities visible to the naked eye. G-d purposely obscured His presence in order for us to use our independence and freedom of choice to reveal it.

When we choose to meditate and become mindful of G-d, we encounter a new "reality" – a world united with G-d, and created, sustained and energized by Him. We begin to see the ultimate purpose and spiritual side of all matter as well as our own role within creation.

At first, it may seem difficult to know G-d. However, G-d provided man with the mental and emotional tools to know Him. He gave us an intellect with which to meditate about Him, a heart with which to feel Him, a mouth with which to speak of Him and eyes to see His design within the world.

When we observe G-d's creations and marvel at the fascinating nature He created within the world, we can begin to discover our Maker and His goodness. It was from His goodness that G-d gave life and existence to the world and creatures.

He gave us a glimpse of His wisdom in the Torah, which guides man on how to lead a purposeful life. He showed us His attributes so that we can emulate Him. We can learn from His qualities of compassion, mercy, kindness and goodness, and act accordingly with others. In reality, G-d is very close to us, concealed within our very beings.

Since the totality of G-d is difficult to comprehend, let alone express or define, many people have a hard time believing in G-d. A story is told about a young rabbi who was seeking to convince a person to fulfill the Torah's commandments. In the midst of the animated discussion, the individual exclaimed: *"But rabbi, I do not believe in G-d."* The rabbi responded: *"You know, the God you don't believe in, I also don't believe in."*

The mere fact that a person attempts to fully understand G-d is problematic, since this attempt is based on a person's limited perception and knowledge. No mind is capable of accurately defining G-d, since any description of Him would be subjective. Man is but a creation of G-d (albeit the most sophisticated) and can never come close to the knowledge of his Maker. Any human conception of G-d is only an invention of the mind. From our human vantage point, we are only capable of seeing things in terms of cause and effect. G-d, whose existence in contingent upon no other existence and who created all matter from nothing, cannot be described or understood in terms of cause and effect. To fully comprehend G-d would necessitate being His equal.

There is a well-known saying of the Sages that states the following[103]: *"The ultimate of knowing You is not to know You."*

In general "not knowing" is seen as a negative condition, since it implies lack of perception and mindfulness. Yet the belief in G-d doesn't necessitate knowledge or understanding, as faith is grounded in the spiritual rather than being con the intellectual. "To know" however, is considered a quality of growth and purpose. In truth, there exist two types of "not knowing," one that is below the conscious and the other that is above.

At the human level, developing the mental faculties necessary to absorb knowledge is the most important advancement one should seek. However, since G-d is infinite, knowing Divinity transcends our mental powers and abilities.

Although reasoning and understanding are signs of personal achievement, at times they can restrict the manifestation of the unlimited potential we have. Accordingly, the words *"the ultimate in knowledge is not to know"*, mean that a person must recognize that, as a limited being, having a full understanding of G-d is unthinkable; For G-d is beyond all limitations. This is in keeping with an all too familiar adage that states: *"the more you know, the more you realize how little you know"*.

Implicit within this statement of the Sages is the idea that when an individual fully broadens his spiritual being, he can tap into the infinite dimensions that normally transcend intellectual comprehension.

We must make ourselves receptive to G-d by freeing ourselves from any mental or spiritual boundaries and approach Him with a faith that transcends our intellectual faculties. With self-transcendence, we are brought to a level of "not knowing" - an infinite closeness to G-d.

Following G-d's Torah and performing acts of kindness bring us closer to G-d. As a matter of fact, the greatest good is the one we perform independent of our rationale or sense of "rightness". When we act out of kindness rather than obligation, we are fulfilling G-d's expectations of us. Through our compassion, we express faith in G-d's reasoning for prescribing the act itself. Emphasizing the genuine kindness of our motivations does not diminish our need to understand the act, as understanding enables us to perform good deeds with deeper feeling and in the best manner possible. G-d is only accessible through the wisdom He shares with us. By studying His wisdom, learning His ways and doing His Will, we connect to and thus know G-d. Consequently, by knowing G-d we become His partner and representative within creation.

Ultimately, we can look forward to the era of Messiah when *"Man will no longer teach his friend, for all will know Me, from the small to the great[104]."*

G-d's creation of the universe was inspired by His desire to dwell within it. A dwelling is a place where our personality is expressed and felt with all of our senses. So too, G-d's motive in creation was that He be obvious within the physical world.

Chapter 23
Creation

Concerning the act of creation, the Torah uses the word "Behabra'am" (Genesis ch.2, v.4). On this word which is similar in meaning and in spelling to the name "Abraham", the Sages comment that the whole of Creation was made for the sake of Abraham's enlightening of the world with his wisdom.

The Torah opens with the words[105]: *"In the beginning, G-d created the heaven and the earth...and G-d's breath hovered upon the surface of the waters."* The Torah continues: *"G-d said, 'Let there be light' and there was light."* Then, *"G-d said, 'let there be a firmament"*, and so on.

These biblical verses teach us important lessons about meditation. Firstly, just as we use breathing to initiate meditation, G-d used breathing in His act of creation. Secondly, G-d imbued creation with light prior to creating the details of worldly existence. It is this G-dly light which we attempt to bond with when meditating on physical existence. Furthermore, we clearly see that G-d used the power of speech to create the world. Speech in the form of Mantras is common practice in many meditative circles.

In the first verse of the Torah, the word for "the" is "et" in Hebrew – a two-letter word comprised of the first and last letter of the Hebrew Alpha Bet, Aleph, and Taf. Jewish Sages explain that the letters of the Torah's Hebrew Alpha Bet were G-d's instruments in creating the physical world[106].

It is said[107]: *"With Ten Utterances the world was created."* The Ten Utterances were mantras of a sort, used to create and maintain the existence of the world. Just as with mantra meditation, the repetition of meaningful words, phrases, verses or paragraphs create a stream of energy to fill the mind and body, in much the same way that G-d's Ten Utterances continually fill the universe with Divine energy and sustenance.

In Psalms[108] it is written: *"Forever, O' G-d, your words stand firm in the heavens."* This verse is explained to mean "your words", i.e. the words that G-d uttered *"Let there be a firmament in the midst of the waters...*[109]*"* stand "firm" and "forever" in heaven. The Ten Utterances of the Torah, the language G-d used to create the world, forever remain the life force of the world.

The spiritual power that allows any entity to exist out of absolute nothingness must be continuous. According to Judaism, G-d is found within the physical world, constantly creating and energizing everything within it with life and vitality. Accordingly, "awareness" or "mindfulness" means being conscious of G-d's constant presence and engagement within creation.

This idea of G-d's continual creation and energizing of the world applies not only to all perishable entities that only exist as their species reproduce, but to inanimate substance such as stone and metal as well. The life force emanating from Above must be vested within them to ensure their continued existence.

For each entity there exists a Hebrew name spoken by G-d that affects its existence. Although not all creations are mentioned in the Ten Utterances, through the combination and substitutions of the letters found in the Ten Utterances we can find the Hebrew name for every creation. In Jewish thought, if the creative Hebrew letters were to depart from any creature for even one moment, the affected creature would return to absolute nothingness as it was before the six days of creation.

Likewise, our own holy words of prayer and Torah study were given a powerful ability to purify and elevate our minds and bodies, as well as the environment we live in.

There are those who believe that G-d created the world from nothing, "ex nihilo", but deny G-d's continued involvement within the world. They maintain that G-d cannot involve Himself within the physical world, since this would cause G-d to lower Himself from His great spirituality. Rather, they believe that creation came about through a downward cause and effect sequence of events. As such, they do not believe in Divine Providence, heavenly signs or miracles that alter the course of nature.

In Tanya[110], Rabbi Schneur Zalman responds to these people. He explains that they come to this conclusion because they compare G-d's creation of the world to the work and methods of man. When a silversmith completes a vessel for example, it no longer relies upon the smith who made it. The vessel remains in exactly the same image and shape as it was originally crafted. Likewise, they believe that G-d's creations remain stagnant and can exist independently.

According to Rabbi Schneur Zalman, however, comparing G-d's creations with man's creations is erroneous at best. Unlike the creations of G-d that sprung from nothingness, any newly shaped object designed by man already existed in potential. Raw metal, for example, can be stretched, bent and shaped into different forms with the aid of fire. Since G-d's creations only came into existence upon His word, they must depend upon Him for sustained existence and constant recreation.

Nevertheless, G-d's involvement in the world does not cause Him to lower Himself. In the Kabbalah, it is said that G-d created the universe via "tzimtzumim" - progressive condensations of His Eternal Light. These spiritual contractions allow G-d to enter this mundane world and provide every recipient with the specific life giving and sustaining G-dly light it needs to exist. Too much spiritual light could cause a recipient to lose its identity and be nullified from existence. When meditating on creation, it is this hidden G-dly light found in all entities which we seek in order to experience enlightenment.

In this process of tzimtzumim, there are five central categories referred to as the "five worlds". These five worlds are further subdivided into myriad gradations, each consisting of domains of their own. In the teachings of Chasidism, these worlds are described as Divine garments in which G-d's Eternal Light conceals and clothes itself to allow matter to come into existence.

The five realms involved in the process of creation are:

"Adam Kadmon"- the Primordial Man. It is also called the "lucid and luminous light" and refers to the innermost Divine Will.
"Atzilut"- World of Emanation. At this level, since only the light of G-d is revealed, no entities can survive. This level is also referred to as that of the encompassing mind.
"Beriyah"- World of Creation. It is the abode of angels and of souls prior to their descent into physical bodies. This stage is also called that of the Divine thought.
"Yetzirah"- World of Formation. This is where the initial signs of entities begin to manifest themselves. This plane is often compared to speech, since speech usually precedes any physical action.
"Asiyah"- World of Action. This is where the soul is embodied within a physical body. Within this realm exist four levels: inorganic matter, vegetation, the animal kingdom and human beings. This world is known as the world of "action" since it is the only world that encompasses physical activity.

Interestingly, Hinduism also speaks of five levels pertaining to the evolution of creation[111]. In the Vedic scriptures it speaks of: 1) "Purusa"- the cosmic man - similar to "Adam Kadmon"; 2) "Garbha" - the cosmic embryo - containing the totality of creation prior to any creative differences, akin to "Atzilut" since at this level, only Divine light exists removed from any form of existence; 3) "Creation" comparable to "Beriyah"; 4)"Ambhas" / "Salila," the realm associated to "Vac", the master of speech, is similar to Yetzirah that is also connected to speech; and 5) "Tad Ekam" - the ultimate source of creation of the earth, is like "Asiyah", where the four categories of life discussed above come into being in a physical way.

In short, G-d provided us with a physical world filled with His Presence even though His light is often concealed or invisible to us. The Baal Shem Tov once said: *"I can bear the fact that G-d chose to be concealed. But what troubles me is when His concealment is also concealed."* Regardless, each part of the universe possesses this light often referred to as a G-dly spark. Through meditations aimed at uniting with the Divine, we discover His greatness within the confinements of our material world.

When one travels to a foreign country, it is important to learn the language of its residents. Similarly, when one communicates with G-d, it is important to articulate our wishes in the way He desires. Even though G-d can understand our needs without them being expressed, with "prayer", our intentions and words expressed from the heart are guaranteed to resound loudly in the lofty realms and bring results.

Chapter 24
Prayer

According to the Jewish tradition, Prayer, like most mitzvoth, must be conveyed in a physical manner – with actual verbal articulation. Nonetheless, we still may consider prayer to be a meditative exercise.

Prayer is often defined as the outpouring of the soul, as it requires "Kavanah" - proper feeling, dedication and focus. In fact, the word Kavanah is deduced from the Hebrew root word "kaven" which means to aim and focus. Rabbi Aryeh Kaplan[112] translates Kavanah as a "direct consciousness". When possessing Kavanah, we permit the Divine act of prayer or the performance of any mitzvah to directly enter our consciousness. The Tanya sees Kavanah as a form of "dvekut", focus on uniting with G-d.

Together, prayer and dvekut elevate our words of prayer to the spiritual realms. The meaningful words of prayer are the inner expression of the soul, while meditation and the devotion of prayer serve to vitalize and carry the message to heaven. It is said[113]: *"Prayer without Kavanah is akin to a body without a soul."* Just like the body cannot survive without its soul, so too, prayer without the proper focus cannot pierce the realms above.

It is thought that by creating a physical world consisting of many separate entities, G-d's presence became concealed and our unity with Him less strong. According to an ancient Kabbalah teaching, however, prayer together with Kavanah reunites and repairs the original Divine Unity that existed prior to the creation of the world.

The Jewish requirement is to pray three times daily. The practice of fixed times for prayer originated with Abraham. The Morning Prayer is called "Shacharit", the afternoon prayer is called "Mincha" and the evening prayer is called "Maariv". It is said that our forefathers instituted these three prayers. Abraham taught us Shacharit, the Morning Prayer; Isaac established

Mincha, the afternoon prayer; and Jacob instituted Maariv, the evening prayer.

While praying Shacharit in the morning, a Jew wears "tefillin" – (phylacteries made of animal hide) - on the head and the arm. The reason the phylacteries are worn on our head and the biceps of our left arm (next to our hearts) is to remind us to subjugate our intellect and emotions to the service of our Creator. Also, a talit with tzitzit - (prayer shawl with its traditional strings tied to its corners) - is worn to recall G-d's infinite light drawn through the 613 Divine commandments of the Torah. We can remember this by noticing that the word tzitzit, when spelled in Hebrew, has the numerical value of 600, and together with its 8 strings that are attached to the shawl and its 5 knots, equals 613. The proper Kavanah or intention behind the wearing of tefillin and talit with tzitzit arouses G-d's presence and ensures the awakening we strive for through performance of mitzvoth.

Maimonides writes that beseeching G-d reinforces the principle that man must recognize G-d as the Master of the Universe[114]. Our faith is nurtured by our affirmations that G-d sees us and involves Himself in our personal lives.

Prayer is also a time of self-evaluation. Prior to beseeching G-d for our needs and desires, it is valuable for us to examine ourselves and to see if we are fit to make such requests.

If we will humble ourselves, we realize that perhaps we do not deserve the favors we are asking of G-d. Therefore, during our prayers we constantly emphasize G-d's infinite kindness and mercy. We beseech G-d to give us our desires even though we are unworthy of them. In this respect, "Tefillah" - (the Hebrew word for prayer) - may also be read as the verb "Pallel" which means to "evaluate oneself". Prior to and during prayer, we should meditate on arousing G-d's infinite kindness, as well as making ourselves worthy of it.

G-d gave us a glimpse of His wisdom within the confines of the Torah, which serves to complete the process of creation and guide us in the establishment of a dwelling place for His essence. When G-d gave the Ten Commandments, He spoke in the first person, for His message was intended for every person in particular. Pay attention, for G-d is talking to you!

Chapter 25
Bonding to G-d via Torah & Mitzvoth

The Talmud (Baba Batra, p.16b) tells us that Abraham had a daughter named Bakol, and in her merit, he was able to observe the entire Torah prior to its enactment seven generations later. The Sages explain that due to her aura, Abraham's house was constantly filled with Divine energy, always open and befitting to all people. The Zohar teaches that Bakol refers to the Shechina - the revelation of G-d's spirit (discussed in ch.21) - which permeated Abraham's being because of his great generosity and loftiness.

However, G-d's greatest revelation occurred on the 6th day of Sivan[122] in the spring of the 2448th year from Creation - (corresponding to 1312 BCE) - when G-d revealed Himself on Mount Sinai in the presence of the entire Jewish Nation. Several million men, women and children witnessed the momentous historical event, the giving of the Torah.

Most people know the story of the Ten Commandments when Moses was given two stone tablets on Mount Sinai. In fact, 613 commandments were given to Moses on that historically significant day. The Torah, which commences with the Five Books of Moses, was not given as a simple history book to recount stories and revelations of the past. The Torah was given to enhance the life of every person in every generation. It has not become outdated even in our modern times.

The Torah also encompasses the subsequent fourteen books of prophets and five additional books of scripture. Even the oral traditions, which were transcribed centuries later, were transmitted to the Jewish People at Mount Sinai. These include the Mishnayot, Talmud and The Kabbalah, the writings of their commentators, and even any further explanations we discover now.

In the Torah, we find both practical instructions and narratives. While most traditional authorities believe the narratives and stories recorded in the Torah to be about events that actually took place, some regard these narratives as symbolism and allegory highly effective in the teaching of G-d's service. According to Chassidic thought, the stories of the Torah relate largely to the spiritual realms, but allude to actual events in our lower world. This means that the Torah's narratives are depictions of the relationships between the Divine attributes above and because the physical world is a consequence of its spiritual counterpart, the events that occur within this world reflect what has taken place above.

The word "Torah" is also associated with the Hebrew word "hora'ah" - meaning "teachings". The teachings of the Torah are meant to guide us through every chapter of our lives, from the time we are born to the day we die. According to Judaism, life without Torah is unthinkable. A well known Professor named Solomon Schechter would tell a story of a priest whose pagan enemies one day beheaded him. Being the good person that he was, he took his head under his arm and left the premises. "You think this is funny" or "too much of a miracle" he would ask to his listeners; He then would say "Judaism without a Torah is even a greater miracle, since this would be a headless Judaism".

Yet the Torah is accessible to all people. G-d provided all of mankind with the Torah as a means of uniting with Him. Essentially, by embodying His wisdom within the confines of the Torah, G-d made Himself available to every human being. The Torah is more than a transcendent spirituality. With the giving of the Torah, G-d provided all of humanity with the power to live a holier and more meaningful life.

Concerning the creation of the world, the Zohar teaches: *"The Holy One Blessed is He looked into the Torah and created the world. When occupying oneself with Torah, the world is maintained."* The Torah is not only the source of all Creation, but even more so, it is man's guidebook to assuring the world's continued survival. Man's thoughts must be imbued with a consciousness of G-d's wisdom as expressed in His Torah.

When we grapple to understand G-d's wisdom, we reach enlightenment. By embracing the Torah with our minds and living by its wisdom physically, we are in fact grasping G-dliness. When we meditate on the Torah, our mind envelops and absorbs Divine wisdom at the same time as the Divine wisdom envelops our minds, uniting our souls with our Maker[123].

Yet, our minds only envelop any intellectual endeavor in stages. Initially, we familiarize ourselves with a deep subject by observing its outer parameters and dimensions. After we have been introduced to the subject, our minds slowly absorb all of its nuances through intense concentration and mental exertion. Upon contemplation, a subject is intertwined with ideas that already exist within our minds, and thus becomes an integral part of our thinking.

When the subject being acquired is Torah, we are actually grasping Divine wisdom, causing it to become part of our thinking. This is how the words of the Torah and wisdom of G-d become one with our being.

In the teachings of Chassidism, it is explained that when we embrace the Torah with our minds, the Divine light of the "Ein Suf" is drawn down at two levels. One light permeates our souls and the other envelops and encompasses our soul. The deeper and more thorough our comprehension is of the Divine wisdom, the more powerful the light will be.

The Torah is often compared to the "bread that nourishes the soul". For the Torah to nourish our souls, it must be digested and internalized just as the bread that nourishes the body. This takes place when we labor to comprehend the Torah to the point where it becomes united with our thoughts. This necessitates deep meditation and proper concentration.

The 613 mitzvoth, the Divine precepts of the Torah, are called the "garments of the soul" because they affect our external functions and abilities. The mitzvoth include 248 positive commandments and 365 prohibitions. The Jewish religion is not just a scheduled religious focus, but also a complete guide to every part of our lives. Each "mitzvah" is defined by specific rules and regulations found in "halacha" - the Jewish code of law.

The Sages of the Talmud[124] point out that the human body is also made up of 613 limbs and blood vessels and that every time a mitzvah is performed, the corresponding bodily organ is elevated. Thus, through the mitzvah of studying Torah, our minds are elevated, and through the mitzvah of wearing the hand tefillin (used during the morning prayers), our arms are elevated. With the mitzvah of charity, the entire body is elevated because the whole body labored to earn the money given to charity.

As previously stated, the word "mitzvah" is also similar to the Hebrew word "tzavta", which means united or joined together, referring to our connecting to G-d. By observing the mitzvoth, we are elevated and we establish an increasingly deeper bond with G-d.

Since our G-dly soul has been enclothed within a human body and lives a material life, the soul's channels for communication with G-d must be elicited through physical means.

Through the performance of mitzvoth that are grounded in our physical expressions of speech, thought and action, our souls and bodies are wholly united with G-d. Thus, when we meditate and focus on the depth of the Torah through "thought", when we articulate the meaning of the mitzvoth through "speech", and when we observe the commandments through "action", the soul unites the body with G-d.

Every mitzvah connects its associated material object to Divinity. By inspiring an associated physical act, the mitzvoth that pertain to emotions such as love, fear and joy of G-d express themselves with material consequences.

In the Jewish tradition, it is believed that G-d's intention in creating the world was to make it a dwelling place for Him. Seeking to go beyond this physical and material world in order to connect to Him would contradict this intent.

With the Torah as an instruction manual for daily living, we have been equipped with the tools to draw G-dliness into the world through physical means without having to seek separation from our mundane body. However, the initiation must come from G-d.

This may be understood by the example found in the teachings of Chassidism[125] regarding the first contact between a simpleton and an intellectual. The simpleton is so undistinguished that he doesn't even realize how ignorant he is. In the mind of the intellectual whose whole life is surrounded with abstract ideas and great wisdom, the simpleton does not even exist. However, if the intellectual happens to need a mundane favor and he asks the simpleton for help, the intellectual has now bridged the gap and initiated a relationship with him.

The simpleton now is of interest to the intellectual, while the intellectual has become part of the simpleton's life. What the intellectual requests is not relevant. What is important, however, is that a demand has been made and that the simpleton has consented to fulfill it.

Similarly, by providing man with "mitzvoth", G-d has "reached down" into the physical world, affording man the opportunities to bond with Him. By relating to Him through the performance of these commandments, we are capable of influencing our environment in a positive way; transforming and elevating every entity G-d has created. Thus, every mitzvah performed solidifies our relationship with G-d and brings mankind as a whole to a higher level of spirituality.

Indeed, mitzvoth are referred to as "seeds" in the verse, *"Sow for yourselves for charity[126]"*. Like a planted seed, every mitzvah we fulfill has the ability to produce a sublime energy within our material world, which, when cultivated and cared for, will blossom into permanent fruit bearing achievements.

G-d gave importance to these edicts in order to give us a way to relate to Him. By fulfilling the mitzvoth, we not only elevate our own being, but also our environment and the entities used in connection with the "mitzvah".

Thus, through the meditation on and physical observance of mitzvoth, an abundant flow of light is drawn into the physical world. In Judaism, a meditation oriented toward detaching the physical from the spiritual is considered incomplete. Any meditation must begin with a thought and conclude with an action. Although G-d desires the service of the heart and mind, if we were to meditate on the "Shema[127]" prayer with deep feelings of love and fear and not verbally recite the words of the Shema, we would not have fulfilled our obligation.

We have the option to obey or disregard the mitzvoth. Yet, by opting to obey, we affirm our connection to G-d. G-d initiated His entry into our world as well as a relationship with us by affording us with mitzvoth, the "spiritual seeds" which awaken the hidden powers within material matter. When fulfilling our spiritual duty of performing mitzvoth, not only do we complete our personal mission in life, but we also help the animal, organic and inorganic kingdoms reach their Divine purpose of existence. Every mitzvah has the ability to awaken the "Divine spark" latent within the utilized matter.

In Tanya[128], Rabbi Schneur Zalman explains that the fulfillment of mitzvoth unites the spiritual world of "Atzilut" - (emanation) - and the worlds of Beriyah - (creation), Yetzirah - (formation) and Asiyah - (action). This is clear when we consider that the essence of all mitzvoth is derived from the realm of Atzilut. The Kabbalah further explains that G-d created these four worlds in order to condense His light so that it may fill the world with vitality[129].

As part of the morning prayers, Jewish mystics of centuries ago included the following declaration: *"(I am doing this) For the sake of the union of the Holy One Blessed be He, with His Shechina, on behalf of all Israel*[130].*"*

Making this statement each morning reminds us of the importance to meditate on the *"union of the Holy One Blessed be He, with His Shechina"* every time we perform a mitzvah. The term "Kudesha Berich Hu" (Holy One Blessed be He) is an Aramaic term representing the hidden aspect of the "Ein Sof". The "Shechina", which literally means "that which Dwells", refers to the Divine Presence of G-d the Creator, who rests wherever there is holiness. For example, the "Shechina" rested in the Holy Temple in Jerusalem.

The significance of this meditation on the above mentioned union runs deeper. The word "holy" - (kedusha) - is usually used to refer to something or someone dedicated to G-d but separate and apart from the earthly matter. Thus, when ascribing G-d as the "Holy One", we are in fact saying that He is completely beyond the mundane. The word "blessed" - (berich) - when referring to G-d, alludes to another associated word "hamavrich", which is interpreted as "drawing down."

Consequently, when we say *"I am doing this in the name of the Holy One Blessed be He"*, we are declaring that G-d, who is absolutely beyond human reach, is nonetheless drawn into the material realm through our fulfillment of His commandments. This therefore bridges the gap between the utterly transcendent and the totally non-spiritual.

The Zohar explains that the Shechina, which is originally found at the final level of the highest spiritual world, namely, "Atzilut", also acts as the starting point for the next world "Beriyah". From there onward, the "Shechina" descends continuously until it reaches the physical world, embodying itself into Torah and mitzvoth.

On the biblical words *"And you shall make for me a dwelling so that I may dwell (in Hebrew, veshachanti) amongst you"*, the commentators explain that this is an eternal message telling us to make the physical world into a habitation for G-d. That is, our every mitzvah act should have as its goal the bringing of G-d's "Shechina" into the world. The world is often seen as sheker, a false one. With the holiness of the "Shechina", however, a transcendent light is drawn into this world transforming the "sheker" - (falseness) - into a "kesher", a "bond," between this dormant world and G-d.

Mitzvah Exercise

In the following exercise, we suggest choosing a mitzvah, an act of goodness you are comfortable with (For example: Give to charity, do someone a favor or visit someone who is sick). At a practical level, try to learn about, understand and perform one mitzvah every day. Keep track of the effect the mitzvah has on you and on the person you are reaching out to. Remember, the effect of the mitzvah is more enduring than the pleasure we personally experience by fulfilling it, since it draws G-dly energy into your life.

> *Relax, sit back and think for a few moments about G-d's utter transcendence.*
>
> *Empty yourself of personal concerns to make yourself a pure receptacle for Divinity.*
>
> *Visualize that you are about to draw G-d's essence into your own person through the act (mitzvah) you are about to perform.*
>
> *Keep in mind that G-d's presence is very real, even though it is not always visible.*
>
> *Deeply appreciate the value of the mitzvah you are performing. Be aware of how, by performing the*

mitzvah, you have become an instrument of Divine intent.

Contemplate the positive influence you have on others and your environment, being most aware of G-d's involvement in your life.

Now, fulfill the act. As you do so, feel G-d's presence being integrated into your own being. Sense the G-dly energy flowing through your body, mind and soul.

The Torah and the mitzvoth were intended to be mankind's media for drawing G-dly light into the world. Although mitzvoth can be performed without prior meditation or the correct Kavanah, its quality and impact will differ substantially. When you perform a mitzvah without the proper mental intention, you have still accomplished a good deed. However with Kavanah and meditation, the performance of mitzvoth will strengthen your connection to G-d as you draw His infinite G-dly energy into the world.

Ever since the birth of civilization, people of all walks of life have wished to experience a reality beyond the confines of the material world. While some have attempted to escape physical reality, others have remained imprisoned by the frontiers of their physical existence. Through the performance of Mitzvoth, we are given the opportunity to bridge the gap between the material and the spiritual, thus elevating our environment and ourselves. Do a Mitzvah today and change the world for a better tomorrow!

Chapter 26
Individual Mitzvoth

The mitzvoth of the Torah are often referred to as "luminaries", as their purpose is to bring light into the world. Their fulfillment varies according to their nature. Generally, the mitzvoth are divided into three categories: "Mishpatim" - (ordinances), "Eidut" - (precepts) and "Chukim" - (statutes). These categories span the spectrum of human understanding and thus require diverse meditations.

Mishpatim, interpreted as civil laws, are the ordinances that appeal to natural human reasoning. These include the laws of fairness, morality, and modesty without which our society would break down and fall into decay. We know that we ought to prohibit murder, kidnapping and adultery. Many of these codes of behavior are mirrored in the animal kingdom. For example, we may learn modesty from the behavior of a cat stealing from a weasel and so on.

Eidut are precepts that we can understand once they are explained to us. These include the mitzvoth that commemorate significant events that occurred throughout Jewish history. They are full of symbolic wisdom, but are not usually actions we would choose to carry out without G-d asking us to. For example, the detailed celebration of Passover is meant to remind us of our historic exodus from ancient Egyptian slavery. On a more practical level, each day and every environment has its correspondent of "slavery", a force which seeks to threaten our freedom of mind, body and soul. The Passover festival and its rituals symbolize our constant efforts to live freely. Another example is the wearing of "tefillin", phylacteries made of animal hide on our head and our arm close to our hearts to remind us to subjugate our intellect and emotions to the service of our Creator. As well, tefillin helps us fill our hearts and minds with G-dliness.

Chukim are statutes that are beyond human and rational understanding, although with adequate consideration, most ultimately reinforce human kindness, respect and purity. By and large however, we obey this third category only because it is G-d's will. These include mitzvoth such as the prohibition against wearing clothes made from a mixture of wool and linen, the prohibition against eating the fruit of a tree less than four years old. Most prominent, the cleansing of the spiritually unclean through the ashes of the Red Heifer, a ritual which was practiced during the days when the Temple stood in Jerusalem. A person becomes spiritually unclean when he or she comes in contact with a dead person. To purify these people, a totally red heifer had to be found, sacrificed and completely burnt. The ashes of this heifer had the power to purify the spiritually unclean. However, inexplicably, the very person who prepared this sacrifice was rendered spiritually unclean.

Each type of mitzvoth has unique qualities. Mishpatim and Eidut allow a person to connect to G-d through reason, understanding and symbolism. Chukim require us to bond with G-d only through faith. According to the Sages, one's ultimate goal is to perform the Mishpatim and Eidut with the same faith we have while doing Chukim and to carry out the Chukim with the same feeling and satisfaction as we do Mishpatim and Eidut.

Perhaps the most mysterious of the mitzvoth are the Chukim. Regarding Chukim, King Solomon said[131]: *"I was able to comprehend all the difficult passages of the Torah. Regarding the Red Heifer, however, I asked and I sought; I said, 'I will become wise,' but I then [saw] that it was far from me."*

However, the Midrash tells us that Moses was privileged with this understanding. *"The Holy One told him: 'To you alone will I reveal the understanding for the Red Heifer[132]'."*

Thus, the Red Heifer is not completely above reasoning since G-d did reveal its reasoning to Moses. On the other hand, since Moses could not teach it to others, even King Solomon, the wisest among men, was not able to grasp it, the Red Heifer must transcend normal human understanding.

G-d's giving of the Torah was not solely motivated by His desire to be obeyed. The Torah was given to help us develop physically and spiritually. That is why G-d made it possible for His Divine wisdom to become part and parcel of the human mind. In this respect, the majority of the Torah is comprised of ideas and thoughts that may be understood intellectually.

Nonetheless, since the Torah is G-d's wisdom and His wisdom is infinite, it cannot all be understood by the human mind. The category of Chukim highlights this fact.

The true acknowledgment of the superiority of G-d's will and His ultimate wisdom is manifested only in our unconditional compliance with all of His mitzvoth. When we achieve this point of acceptance, the mind is elevated to a level beyond understanding.

This concept is illuminated in Rashi's writings on the Torah portion[133] that speaks of the Red Heifer. Rashi quotes the Sages of the Talmud[134]: *"It is a decree before me, and you have no right to speculate upon it."*

Perhaps it would have been more appropriate if the Sages had stated: *"you have no right to disobey it"*, instead of *"to speculate upon it"*?

These words hint to the fact that limiting the mitzvah to only the physical act is insufficient. Instead, the elevation of the mind must follow. This implies that one should not only not doubt the words of G-d, but that faith beyond understanding should fill the mind, until there is no room for any speculation.

If the whole Torah were understandable, then we would be limited to the capacity of our own minds when pursuing the wisdom of G-d. Our actions would, likewise, be limited to our own mental restrictions. Facing spiritual challenges would be difficult, since we would be constantly rationalizing our behavior and thus never really breaking away from the mental barriers we have created.

With mitzvoth, like the Red Heifer however, we are filled with enlightenment by the infinite quality of the Torah and this motivates us to fully accomplish higher spiritual goals.

The category of Eidut, with all of its symbolism, meaning, and wisdom, is probably the group most appropriate to the practice of meditation. Special thoughts and feelings can be aroused with commemorative mitzvoth that take us back in time to special events and revelations which occurred throughout Jewish history.

We will sample some mitzvoth that fall into the category of Eidut to offer the reader a feeling of their nature.

The holiday of Passover commemorates the Jewish People's historic redemption from slavery in Egypt. One of the themes of the Passover holiday is the idea that we must always be moving forward beyond our individual limitations. This is implicit in the name "Passover". In Hebrew, "Pesach" (Passover) literally means to "leap over". Moreover, the Hebrew name "Mitzrayim" (for Egypt) also means "limitations". When we celebrate the Mitzrayim of Passover, we at the same time celebrate our ongoing departures from our own limitations, temptations and obstructions which physical life places before us.

To experience this feeling of personal freedom from our limitations, we are commanded to eat the "matzah" (unleavened bread) for seven days. "Matzah", which is flat, symbolizes the importance of being humble and free from arrogance. When we have made efforts to humble ourselves, freedom from our personal obstacles becomes possible. On the other hand, the prohibited "leavened bread", referred to in Hebrew as "chametz", bloats while rising and is symbolic of self-inflated pride and egoism. Like the leavened bread during Passover, these qualities should be avoided.

According to the Zohar[135], "matzah" is also called the "bread of faith", since it represents faith beyond limitations and rational intellect.

During the month of April, starting from the second day of Passover, the Torah tells us to count forty-nine days until the holiday of Shavuot, which commemorates the giving of the Torah. This counting reminds us of the time when the Jews were freed from Egyptian bondage and anxiously counted the days until they would reach spiritual perfection in order to receive the Torah on Mount Sinai.

Today, our counting also testifies to the importance of improving our character traits. Each of the forty-nine days corresponds to a different personal character trait that should be perfected through careful contemplation. On the first day of the counting, we recite mystical words that assist us in perfecting our trait of kindness; on the second day we refine the quality of stringency, and so on[136].

On Rosh Hashanah, the Jewish New Year, we blow the "shofar" (a ram's horn) for two reasons. As with the sounding of trumpets in the presence of a King, the sound of the shofar proclaims G-d as the king and master of the universe. Unlike a trumpet, the shofar sounds similar to the cries of a human being and serves to remind us that we must always improve ourselves and return to G-d.

On "Yom Kippur", the Day of Atonement, we fast and dress in white to encourage ourselves to behave like heavenly angels and to help us keep our prayers and meditations pure and sincere.

The holiday of Sukkot commemorates the Jewish People's travels in the desert after leaving Egypt. The Torah urges us to build a Sukkah (a wooden hut) and to dwell within it for seven days. The Sukkah totally surrounds us with a mitzvah, providing us with the opportunity to elevate all aspects of our life. This mitzvah also reminds us that G-d is not limited to a house of worship or to study hall. Rather, the Sukkah confirms that Divinity is found in every dimension and detail. The Sukkah is also symbolic of togetherness as it gathers men, women and children to dwell as one within it.

During the holiday of Sukkot, the Torah tells us to hold together four different plant species and direct them in a specified way. We hold the "Lulav" (palm branch), the "Hadas" (myrtle branch), the "Aravah" (willow branch) and the "Etrog" (citron fruit).

Each of these different species symbolizes a different type of person. The "Etrog" has both a good taste and a pleasant smell. It symbolizes the type of people who have understanding – implicit by its quality of "taste", since in Hebrew the word "taam" (taste) also means understanding. The Etrog also symbolizes people who do mitzvoth, since smell represents the acceptance of the yoke of heaven that usually motivates one to fulfill the precepts of the Torah.

The "lulav," however, represents people who only possess understanding, since the lulav has only taste and no smell. The "Hadas," on the other hand, which has only a pleasant fragrance and no taste, represents those who observe the mitzvoth and do not have understanding. Lastly, the "Aravah", which has no taste or smell, represents individuals who have neither understanding nor fulfillment.

This mitzvah of bonding the four species encourages us to meditate on the intrinsic unity that exists between human beings. No one person can be complete without joining together with others.

Hanukah is often called the Holiday of Lights. During this holiday, we light candles for eight days. This act of kindling the menorah (candle or oil light candelabra) reminds us of the miracle that took place centuries ago when the People of Israel were forced to abandon their faith and their Holy Temple in Jerusalem was violated. When the Jews came to rededicate their temple, they found only one small jar of undefiled oil, enough to supply the temple's menorah for one day alone. Miraculously, the oil lasted for eight days.

The Holiday of Lights is a good time to meditate on the triumph of light over darkness and good over evil. It also urges us to never be satisfied, and to instead constantly increase our measure of light in this world with acts of goodness and kindness, just as we increase the number of lights on the menorah each night of the holiday.

All the mitzvoth we accomplish, and, by extension, every act of goodness, brings us closer to G-d. The 613 mitzvoth are like a rope made up of 613 strands. With each mitzvah we perform, the rope connecting us to G-d becomes firmer. The stronger the rope, the deeper becomes our unity with all of mankind. We are G-d's representatives to whom the vision of making the physical world a meaningful one was given. As we carry out our purposes in life, we at the same time internalize it. We cause an impact on the world at large and become changed ourselves. This happens when our acts of goodness are imbued with the intention of uniting the entire universe in a splendid intimacy with G-d.

17 Sefer Yetzirah quoted in Midrash Says, Bereishit, Benei Yakov Publications, pg. 188

18 Bereishit Rabba, chapter 38:19,see also Midrash Says, Bereishit, Benei Yakov Publications, pg. 120

19 According to the teachings of the Sages, Abraham was tested by G-d with ten trials, each of which brought him to a greater bond with Him. According to Pirkei R. Eliezer, the ten trials Abraham was tested with are: 1) Nimrod's desire to kill Avraham and his hiding in a cave for many years 2) The cauldron of Ur Kasdim. 3) Leaving his home country. 4) The famine he encountered in the land of Canaan. 5) Sarah being taken away by Pharaoh. 6) The battle against the four kings who captured Lot. 7) The covenant with G-d during which Avraham was shown the future exiles of his descendants. 8) The commandment to circumcise himself and his sons. 9) The commandment to send away Hagar and Ishmael. 10) The Akaida – the commandment to offer his son as a sacrifice.

20 A spiritual commune

21 Sotah 10a

22 Shabbat 89b

23 Almost all commentators are of the view that Abraham wrote the Sefer Yetzirah, including the Zohar, Raziel and the 10th century Saadia Gaon. Several of the older copies of The Sefer Yetzirah are prefaced with the words "the letters of Abraham our Father."

24 Pirkei D'Rabbi Eliezer, p48 (Warsaw printing 1852)

25 The Sefer Yetzirah, Rabbi Aryeh Kaplan, Moznaim Publishing Corp. p267

26 Avoda Zarah 14b

27 Ra'avad on The Sefer Yetzirah 6:4

28 Genesis 12:5

29 See Shnei Luchot HaBrit, Torah She Bichtav, Vayeshev (Lvov 1860) 3:65a; Pitchey Teshuvah, Yorah Deah 62:2; see also Yerushalmi, Peah 1:1; Rashi on Genesis 37:2

30 Berachot 55A; Ramban on Exodus 31:3

31 The Torah later states (Exodus 31:2-3) about Betzalel, "and I have filled him with the spirit of G-d with wisdom (chochma), understanding (binah), and knowledge (da'at).

32 Abraham was the first to be called a "Hebrew" (Ivri). We also find that his descendant Joseph was referred to as "the Hebrew" (Genesis 41:12). The name stayed on and the Jewish People became known as "the Hebrews."
33 Shmos Rabbah 12:3
34 Exodus 19:20
35 Exodus 24:1
36 I: 162a
37 Genesis 30:31
38 In short, these rules are: 1) Awareness and devotion to the One Creator G-d of the Universe – this requires meditating and praying to G-d; 2) Honoring G-d and not cursing Him – this means trusting that everything G-d does within the world is for our good, although often this may be concealed; 3) To not murder – this includes recognizing the value of every human being, which according to the Sages, is equivalent to the entire world; 4) Revering the institution of marriage – an echo of G-d's unity with His creation; 5) To not steal – trust instead that G-d will provide us with all our needs; 6) The respect of all creatures – including all animals and species; and 7) Uphold a justice system whereby ethical rules and morality is maintained.

39 Jewish Meditation, Aryeh Kaplan, pg. 40
40 The Rebbe's Advice (Mendelsohn Press, 1998, p. 104)
41 H.H. Bloomfield and R.B. Kory "Happiness" The TM program, Psychiatry and Enlightenment (New York: Simon and Schuster, 1976, p. 143)
42 H.H. Bloomfield, M. Cain and D. Jaffe, TM: Discovering Inner Energy and Overcoming Stress (New York: Delacorte Press. 1975, p. 125)
43 R.K. Wallace, physiological effects of Transcendental Meditation, science (27 March 1970, p. 1751-4,: The Book of Meditation, Patricia Carrington, Element, 1.55)
44 Ibid., The Book of Meditation p. 56
45 See Meditation for Dummies, Stephen Bodian, IDG Books worldwide p. 36
46 Toldos, p.17
47 Chapter 4

End Note

48 Talmud, Baba Metzia 86b
49 Tehillat Hashem prayer book, p.17
50 Tanya, chapter 3
51 In English, "ko'ach" means "strength" or "power."
52 In English, "ma" means "what" or "that."
53 See Tanya, Iggeret Hakodesh, chapter 15
54 See Tanya, Chapter 4
55 Avos 2:1
56 Chapter 6
57 See our chapter on Soul breathing
58 See Tanya chapters 21-22 and 48-49
59 Tractate Megillah, 6:2
60 Koretz 1784 p. 69b or G. Schelm MGWI 77:287. See also Meditation and The Kabbalah by Aryeh Kaplan, published by Samuel Weiser p. 107
61 See Meditation and The Kabbalah p. 108
62 The very first reference to Mechikah is found in the ancient Kabbalah, and is believed to have been practiced since the dawn of man.
63 Tanya, chapter 6
64 Tanya, chapter 50
65 Tanya, chapter 41
66 Quoted in Likkutei Sichot, vol. 3, pg. 987
67 Zohar, Vol.I, p251a
68 Isaiah 10:15
69 Ethics of Our Fathers, chapter 3
70 Genesis 2:7
71 Deuteronomy 12:23
72 Isaiah 11:2
73 Interestingly, the four elements (earth, air, fire and water) used in G-d's creation of the world as described in the Torah, have now been integrated in the practices of many new age religions.
74 Genesis 1:2
75 From Hinduism Back to Judaism, Himelsein Glazerson Publishers, 1990, M. Glazerson, pg. 16
76 In Hebrew, the letters for the "p" and "f" sound are interchangeable.

77 Tanya, chapters 3 & 4
78 Bava Batra, page 9:2
79 Chapter 1
80 Isaiah 6:3
81 Jeremiah 23:24
82 Ecclesiastes 12:1
83 Eichah 3:23
84 Avot 5:23
85 Yoma 38b
86 See chapter on Pain and Suffering
87 Derech Chaim, Shaar Hateshuvah Rabbi Dov Ber of Lubavitch ,ch 9, p. 13 a-b; see also maamar Asher Yei'amar; Or Torah, Parashat Vayeira p.103 and maamar Tzohar Taaseh 5673; and Likkutei Dibburim, Vol. I p. 166
88 Page 50
89 Taanit p. 21 and Sanhedrin p. 108
90 Rashi, Genesis 1:1
91 Genesis 1:35
92 Igeret Hakodesh, ch. 25
93 Zohar I, 27b
94 Tanya, Igeret Hakodesh, ch 22
95 See Likutei Sichos vol. 1 Parshat Noah
96 When counseling friends or acquaintances, one should be very careful. Pain and affliction, usually consequences of illness, material loss, or the loss of a close one are often expressed emotionally.
97 Portion Ki Tetse p.276b
98 Exodus, 20:2
99 Mishna Torah, Hilchos Yesodei HaTorah, chapter 1:1
100 Ibid., chapter 1:3
101 Exodus 3:14
102 See Tanya, Shaar Hayichud Veha'emunah, chapters 1 & 2
103 Bechinos Olam sec. 8 ch. 2; Ikarim, Discourses II, ch. 30 ; Shaloh 191b
104 Jeremiah 31:33
105 Genesis 1:1-4

End Note

106 Interestingly, one may note that the term Alpha Bet also similar to the first and second letters of the Hebrew Alpha Bet – "Aleph" and "Bet."
107 Ethics of Our Fathers, chapter 5, par. 1
108 119:89
109 Genesis 1:6
110 Shaar Ha Yichud Veha'emunah, ch. 2
111 See Part I, ch. 9 of this book for lengthier discussion of this comparison
112 See Jewish Meditation p. 49
113 Shenei Luchot Habrit, vol. I p. 249b or Tanya ch. 38
114 Guide to Perplexed III, ch 36, 44
115 Guide to Perplexed III, ch 36
116 See Philosophy of Chabad, by Nissan Mindel, Kehot Publication Society pg 108
117 Keter Shem Tov pg. 44
118 Tanya, chapters 19 & 46
119 Proverbs 20:27
120 See As for Me My Prayer, by Nissan Mindel, p.6
121 For more precise details, please consult the original essay - particularly chapter twelve.
122 Sivan is the third month of the Jewish calendar, which is based upon the cycles of the moon.
123 See Tanya ch. 5
124 Makkot 24a
125 See Rabbi Yosef Y. Schneersohn of Lubavitch, in "*Hatamim*" Vol. I, 25, Warsaw, 1935, and also Iggrot Kodesh Vol. 10. P. 368
126 Hose'a 10:12
127 An obligatory prayer recited twice daily establishing G-d's unity with His creations. See Siddur Tehillat Hashem p. 46
128 ch. 40
129 See chapter 22 for further discussion of this topic.
130 See Tehillat Hashem, P 30. Tanya ch. 41
131 Ecclesiastes 7:23
132 Tanchuma sec. 8
133 Rashi Numbers 19:2
134 Yoma 67b

135 Vol. II p. 183b
136 See Siddur Tehillat Hashem p. 340